Why Can't HE Be More Like ME?

POPPY SMITH

HARVEST HOUSE PUBLISHERS

EUGENE, OREGON

Unless otherwise indicated, all Scripture quotations are from The Holy Bible, New International Version®, NIV®. Copyright © 1973, 1978, 1984, 2011 by Biblica, Inc.™ Used by permission. All rights reserved worldwide.

Verses marked MSG are from The Message. Copyright © by Eugene H. Peterson 1993, 1994, 1995, 1996, 2000, 2001, 2002. Used by permission of NavPress Publishing Group.

Verses marked TLB are from *The Living Bible*, Copyright © 1971. Used by permission of Tyndale House Publishers, Inc., Wheaton, IL 60189 USA. All rights reserved.

Cover design by Koechel Peterson & Associates, Inc., Minneapolis, Minnesota

Cover photos © iStockphoto / Thinkstock; Hemera / Thinkstock

The author is represented by MacGregor Literary Inc. of Hillsboro, Oregon.

Why Can't He Be More Like Me?
Copyright © 2012 by Poppy Smith
Published by Harvest House Publishers
Eugene, Oregon 97402
www.harvesthousepublishers.com

Library of Congress Cataloging-in-Publication Data
    Smith, Poppy, 1946-
    Why can't he be more like me? / Poppy Smith.
       p. cm.
    ISBN 978-0-7369-4333-8 (pbk.)
    ISBN 978-0-7369-4335-2 (eBook)
    1. Wives—Religious life. 2. Marriage—Religious aspects—Christianity. 3 Man-woman relationships—Religious aspects—Christianity. 4. Smith, Poppy, 1946- I. Title.
    BV4528.15.S67 2012
    248.8'435—dc23

                       2011028815

Printed in the United States of America

12 13 14 15 16 17 18 19 20 / LB-SK / 10 9 8 7 6 5 4 3 2 1

To the only wise God,
the One who knows the end from the beginning
and whose ways are loving and good,
be glory forever through Jesus Christ. Amen.

To Jim, my faithful husband,
who has grown with me in the ups and downs
of the journey called marriage.

Acknowledgments

I owe a debt of thanks to many who supported me in this project:

My agent, Sandra Bishop, of MacGregor Literary Agency for morphing from being my friend to also becoming my agent and believing in the need for this book. Thank you for challenging me to persevere.

To Rod Morris, senior editor at Harvest House Publishers, for your encouraging comments and belief in the value of a book that discusses struggles in marriage.

To my enthusiastic, supportive critique group: Pamela Rosales, Ginnimarie Kennedy, Karen Robbins, and Miriam Cheney. Your prayers, editing skills, and constant affirmation of both the content and my writing, filled me with energy and delight.

Lastly, I thank my husband, Jim, who good-humoredly calls himself "the star" of this book. I admire your willingness to allow me to write truthfully about two imperfect people who remained committed to their marriage vows—and have survived to reap the many rewards of that commitment.

Contents

PART I

This Isn't
What I Expected

One

What Happened to My Dreams?

*He who began a good work in you will carry it
on to completion until the day of Christ Jesus.*

PHILIPPIANS 1:6

Wow! *Who is that?*

Eyeballs bulging, I stared at the stranger striding down the aisle of my small, predominantly British church in Nairobi, Kenya. Well over six feet, tanned, and dressed in a light khaki tropical suit, the man's physical appeal oozed out of him. He sat down, pulled out a small Bible from his pocket, and joined in the singing. I had to meet him.

At twenty years old, I had lived and worked in Nairobi for three years. My parents returned to England two years earlier, when my father's stint with the Royal Air Force in Kenya finished.

My job as secretary to a high-ranking Kenyan in the University of Nairobi kept me busy. I enjoyed friendships with people of various nationalities. And, as a newly converted, somewhat unconventional young woman, I felt embraced by a loving group of older Christians. But, on the rebound from a going-nowhere relationship and with no family to lean on, loneliness consumed me. I longed for someone to belong to.

Watching the good-looking stranger, my mind whirled with excitement: *Who is this man? What is he doing in Nairobi? Has he moved here or is he just passing through? Is he single? How can I get introduced to him? If he is unattached, how can I invite him to our singles' Bible study without looking like I'm interested? Perhaps he is God's answer to my fervent prayer. Maybe he's the one God intends for me.*

So much for worshipping the Almighty! Hymns, prayers, and preaching swirled around me. I was far away on a cloud of dreams and fantasies. I couldn't wait for the service to end.

We did meet that morning, and after a few months, Jim started attending the singles' group when he was in town. He was shy and reserved around me, and I wondered for a year if anything would happen.

Finally, on a day vividly imprinted in my memory, we ran into each other at a local grocery store. Smiling down at me, Jim said, "I've wanted to ask you out. Are you free this Saturday night?"

Bells rang, heaven sang, and the angels celebrated. Right? Well, perhaps, but not for the same reasons I rejoiced. My dreams were coming true. But unknown to me, God had far more significant plans in mind. He intended to use my relationship with Jim to radically transform me into a very different person.

In Philippians, the apostle Paul says, "And I am sure that God who began the good work within you will keep right on helping you grow in his grace until his task within you is finally finished on that day when Jesus Christ returns" (Philippians 1:6 TLB).

God had begun that good work in my life three years earlier when my friends, Rosalyn and Richard, invited me to their home for the weekend. After attending church, Richard asked when I had become a Christian. His question confused me. Wasn't everyone born in England automatically a Christian? By the end of our conversation, however, his explanation of the gospel showed me how far I was from God.

When Richard left me alone with my thoughts, I sat for what seemed like hours thinking about some poor choices I had made. Later that day, troubled by my guilty conscience, I asked God to forgive my sins and help me live in a new way.

Before long, the Holy Spirit made it clear that my colorful language, humorous but hurtful sarcasm, and tendency to flirt with whatever man I found attractive didn't exactly reflect the godly character the Lord desired for me. But these were only surface issues. In order to become who God had in mind, I needed a deep inner transformation. He knew just the circumstance to use: marriage.

Let's Be Honest

Yes, this is a book about marriage. But not the fairy-tale version where we dream of a man with movie-star looks, meet and date this model of perfection, quickly tie the knot surrounded by family and friends who adore him, and live happily ever after in wedded bliss.

This book is not a philosophical treatise on the wonders of the marital union. Nor is it a scriptural exposition of how God intends marriage to picture Christ and His bride, the church.

Instead, this book takes an honest look at the unexpected struggles, disappointments, and choices we wrestle with when our dreams fizzle or shatter into pieces. Its purpose is to encourage you to give your broken dreams to God, discovering how He can use them in ways you never imagined to produce personal and spiritual growth.

This Book Is for You If...

Have you ever listened to talks, watched videos, or read books on marriage that left you discouraged or frustrated and unable to relate? In response to one article where the author wrote about her passionate and creative husband, I wanted to shout, "What about the rest of us? We don't have husbands who jump out of closets, bouquet in hand, delighting us over and over again with their love. Get real!"

If you identify with similar frustrations, if you're married to someone who isn't like you, someone you love but want to strangle at times, this book is for you. If your spouse is someone you cozy up to but clash with often, someone who drives you to tears and fervent prayers for God to help you run away, maybe even someone who can release tense moments between you by making you laugh even when you want to stay mad, this book is for you.

If you're dealing with fizzled dreams, I promise I won't leave you in a painful place, dwelling on what went wrong and stuck in blame and bitterness. We will visit these issues because we need to learn about ourselves, our spouse, and what triggers our flare-ups. But my heart is to provide you with hope and practical help to strengthen your marriage.

Each chapter in this book tackles common frustration-producing issues. You know, the stuff that makes you scream: "How can you think like that? What is the matter with you? Why aren't you normal, like me?"

You'll have an opportunity to reflect on how you and your spouse respond to various situations. You'll also find life-changing scriptural principles you can apply immediately. Like the wise woman described in Proverbs 14:1, you'll learn practical ways to build your relationship rather than tearing it down through negative reactions.

My passionate desire is to help you grow in understanding yourself and the man you married.

My passionate desire is to help you grow in understanding yourself and the man you married. He is not just like you, but God loves him and can work in him, despite his flaws (and yours).

I also pray that you'll ask God to take you to a new level of spiritual maturity as you begin to analyze your relationship, accept the fact that you are two different people, and learn to adapt and appreciate each other.

Let me assure you, if you ask God for wisdom and put His principles for a healthy relationship into practice, positive changes will follow. Perhaps you'll experience fewer angry words, less tension, more grace toward your spouse, a willingness to forgive, or a greater sensitivity to recognizing and releasing bitter feelings.

However, the changes you experience as God works in your heart don't guarantee that your marriage will improve. It takes the willingness of both partners for that to happen. What I can promise is that when you invite God to work in the deepest recesses of your heart, you will benefit regardless of what happens to your marriage.

Dreams Are Made of This

As a young, single doctor in the midsixties, Jim expected to be drafted to Vietnam after he finished his internship. Instead, he found himself on a two-year assignment as a Peace Corps doctor traveling around Kenya keeping Peace Corps agriculture volunteers healthy. He learned to fly, climbed two mountains, and lived in a three-bedroom house with a housekeeper/cook and gardener.

If our courtship in Kenya was any predictor for our future, our marriage looked to be one thrilling adventure after another.

Clambering into Jim's Land Rover one Saturday morning, we drove miles into the bush, his rifle nestled in the backseat. We stopped in an isolated area, and I watched as Jim walked a quarter mile from the vehicle and dropped to one knee. He raised his gun and shot a hulking, gray wildebeest standing two hundred yards away, innocently eyeing him like a curious Jersey cow. I had never seen anyone shoot anything.

After skinning the animal, Jim dragged a hindquarter, along with the skin, back to the Land Rover while vultures circled above. My part was to make spaghetti bolognaise that night using the wildebeest meat. We both agreed the final result smelled and tasted awful.

Jim took me flying in a little Cessna two-seater he rented from a local airport. On one occasion, we almost stalled out as we took off from a high-altitude runway. Jim had forgotten to adjust the fuel mixture. After that near-death experience, I stayed on the ground.

A five-day expedition up Mt. Kilimanjaro topped all the other exciting experiences that came with dating an adventuresome man. Physical activity was never my strength, so I had no idea what I was getting into. But I was twenty-one, in love, and wanting to prove that I shared Jim's interests even if I risked plunging into a glacier or dying from lack of oxygen at nineteen thousand feet.

As it turned out, I did develop altitude sickness at fifteen thousand feet and everyone agreed I needed to descend immediately. While Jim and the others grunted their way to the summit, one of the porters escorted me to a lower hut. Having been trained by the British in the art of "civilized" mountain climbing, he immediately made me some hot tea with milk and sugar and produced a plate of cookies.

A photo of all five of us taken at the end of the climb shows four people with wreaths of everlasting flowers circling their hats. I stood in the middle clutching a posy. Yes, I was the failure of the group, but despite my distinct lack of athletic ability, I must have impressed Jim.

Soon after my brave attempt to conquer Kilimanjaro, Jim proposed. We married a few months later in the small English church where we first met. Neither of us had any family at the wedding, nor had we met each other's parents. Jim had never been to England, and I had never visited America.

Warning Signs

During our month-long traipse through Asia on our way back to the United States, we stopped in Singapore where my parents lived at the time. Thrilled to meet his new son-in-law, my father beamed and pumped Jim's hand enthusiastically. My petite mother, undeterred by Jim's height, reached up, grabbed him by the neck, and pulled him down to her level. She planted a welcoming kiss on his cheek. They were delighted with my new husband—even if he was an American.

A short time later we flew to Iowa where I met my in-laws for the first time. We all shook hands, politely nodding and saying, "Hello." On the way from the airport to their home, we sat in silence. My stomach churned and my mind whirled with questions. *Why aren't they friendly? Why don't they say anything? Are they upset that Jim married me, a girl ten years younger, from another country and a different kind of church?* They never had to say a word for me to sense that I wasn't the woman they had hoped and expected their eldest son to marry.

What Happened to My Dreams?

Arriving in my new country as a starry-eyed bride of twenty-two, I assumed our exciting relationship would become even more thrilling. I imagined Jim and I would stay up late, snuggled on the couch by the fire drinking coffee and looking deeply into each other's eyes. In these tender moments, we would reveal our secret longings and deepest thoughts.

It took me a long time to accept reality: Jim didn't like staying up because he started work early. He didn't drink coffee, and he wasn't a talker.

On weekends, I expected Jim and I would go shopping together. I imagined showing him a pretty blouse and watching his eyes light up as he whispered, "I'd love to see you in that. Don't worry about the price; you're worth it." Of course, that never happened.

Like many men, Jim shops only when necessary. He reluctantly sidles into the men's department, sweeps his eyes over the merchandise, declares there's nothing he likes, and escapes—all in five minutes. Expecting him to stroll through store after store holding my hand and searching for just the right outfit turned out to be as realistic as believing I could run a marathon.

I also assumed that Jim would be like my father, willing to help with the cleaning, ironing, and cooking. When I asked him to mop the kitchen floor, he quickly informed me that in his home, his mother and sister took care of the household chores. Men did the outside work. Roles were not interchangeable.

After our short visit with Jim's parents, we settled in Oregon for the first year of Jim's five-year residency training program. He spent most of his waking hours buried in the hospital, sleeping there every other night as the junior "on-call" resident. When he did stumble home, he buried himself in his studies or fell into bed, exhausted.

> After being married for only six months,
> I felt I had made the worst mistake of my life.

Although I found a job and we regularly attended a small church when Jim was not on call, I had no friends to talk with in the whole country. Disillusioned and overwhelmed once again by painful loneliness, I grew bitter, angry, and hopeless. After being married for only six months, I felt I had made the worst mistake of my life.

What Happened to Your Dreams?

To help you begin to understand your own relationship, let me encourage you to think back. What did you envision for those first few months of marriage? _____

_____

How did you feel about your marriage when some of your dreams fizzled? _____

_____

How would you describe your current feelings? _____

_____

Ignorance Is Bliss. Or Is It?

It never occurred to me that Jim and I would have any problems adjusting to each other. After all, I reasoned, a girl meets a hunky male, her senses go on high alert, her hormones go crazy, and all she wants is to get married and do what comes naturally. In time, she hopes to produce a few adorable babies who complete her other dream, that of the perfect family.

What could be more normal?

The problem is that we expect to marry our clone, someone who is reasonable like us. Someone who sees things our way. Someone whose responses guarantee marital harmony. We reason: Since we love each other, how could marriage be difficult? Or filled with hurt? Or produce heartbreaking disappointment?

> We expect to marry our clone, someone who is
> reasonable like us. Someone who sees things our way.
> Someone whose responses guarantee marital harmony.

We'll explore these understandable assumptions and how they contribute to the fizzling of our fantasies in a later chapter.

Gary Thomas comments on the cultural belief that romantic feelings are the criteria for both marrying and staying married. In *Sacred Marriage* he writes, "The idea that a marriage can survive on romance alone, or that romantic feelings are more important than any other consideration when choosing a spouse, has wrecked many a marital ship.[1]

But that was the basis on which I married. Perhaps you did as well.

Hidden Dream Busters

Neither Jim nor I understood how different backgrounds, beliefs, and personalities could wreck a marriage—even when the marriage is between two committed Christians. Like huge icebergs that reveal only a small part of their powerful ability to rip apart the strongest ships, these issues didn't appear significant at first. But they soon began tearing at our relationship.

Dream Buster 1: Different Backgrounds

We quickly discovered that our backgrounds gave us few experiences or values in common. Jim was raised on a farm in Iowa where life rarely changed. People worked hard, saved their money, and never spent what they didn't have or buy what they didn't need.

Because of my father's career in the British Air Force, I moved every few years from England to various Asian countries and back again to England. My family found change stimulating and exciting. We thrived in different cultures eating local specialties and visiting unusual places. Determined to enjoy the time we had overseas, we also happily spent most of the money my father earned.

Dream Buster 2: Different Beliefs

Our beliefs on spiritual issues and Christian lifestyles also undermined our relationship. Jim was raised by ultraconservative parents who attended a church with many rules. Everyone was expected to conform. Women were not to cut their hair, wear makeup, jewelry, or "men's" clothing. Men with facial hair were frowned on and knew better than to miss a haircut. Watching movies and television or attending sporting events or concerts was of "the world."

Knowing the kind of restrictions I would face as part of his family and church, Jim tried to explain the beliefs and practices that formed his spiritual heritage. But being a young, immature believer whose only exposure to Christians was the loving group that embraced me in Nairobi, I could not grasp the significance of what he said. Nor did I understand how living with these expectations would affect our marriage. I decided I'd deal with whatever was required of me once we arrived in America.

In contrast to Jim's spiritual heritage, my family never attended church. Coming to faith in Christ at the age of seventeen, I had never read the Bible or been taught scriptural principles for living a life that honored God.

The mercy and grace of God was powerfully real to me. But I didn't have any idea how to put my faith into practice when wrestling with shattered dreams.

During my five years in Nairobi as a young believer, I grew to love the Lord deeply. Driving to work each morning, I sang hymns like "Amazing Grace" and "Jesus, Thou Joy of Loving Hearts," barely able to see through my tears of gratitude. The mercy and grace of God was powerfully real to me. But I didn't have any idea how to put my faith into practice when wrestling with shattered dreams.

Although your different beliefs might not create such major rifts between you, they can still become a source of conflict and heartache. A later chapter will address the issue of not being on the same page spiritually. It will also help you find ways to strengthen your marriage in spite of your differences.

Dream Buster 3: Different Personalities

Within a few weeks of settling down together, Jim and I discovered we had polar opposite ways of communicating, handling conflict, spending money, and even relating as husband and wife. Once over the initial shock of how differently we looked at issues, we handled our frustrations the only way we knew how. We copied what our parents did.

When irritated, I reacted in anger and hurled cruel words. If I was particularly infuriated, I slammed doors, threw myself on the bed, and sobbed in frustration. After asking why I was upset and getting no answer that made sense to him, Jim would withdraw, bewildered and wounded by my behavior. Neither of us knew how to respond to the other's pain.

Because negative communication patterns and conflict styles destroy marriages, this book has a chapter on each issue. Learning how to speak positively, even when expressing strong feelings, is essential for changing the atmosphere in a marriage. These chapters will show you how to talk and disagree with each other in ways that draw you together rather than drive you apart.

With my dreams dashed and my naive expectations colliding with real life, I spent the next four years swinging helplessly between anger and despair. I wrestled daily with out-of-control emotions: *Why had I been so stupid, marrying someone I hardly knew? Where was God in this mess? What was I supposed to do?*

Divorcing Jim and starting over with someone else seemed like the best solution. Twenty-five years old and married the rest of my life to someone who wasn't what I expected or wanted was more than I could face.

But divorce was not what God had in mind.

Challenges and Choices

Perhaps divorce does not hover in your thoughts. In fact, you might never have wrestled with the temptation to walk away. Instead, you're looking for a fun and enlightening read that provides both scriptural and practical ways to have the best possible marriage. My prayer is that this book will help you achieve your goal by sparking new and helpful insights into your relationship and spurring you on to become a "wife of noble character" (Proverbs 31:10).

Some of you, however, might be battling the same temptation I faced—to leave and start again.

Seeking Perfection

Recent research indicates that "more than 50 percent of the marriages in the US end in divorce within the first 15 months."[2] Marriages also split in large numbers after the children leave home. This is not what our dreams included at the beginning, but it happens.

When we expect our marriage to make us feel good every day, the temptation to keep searching for the "perfect" partner is powerful. But our quest for perfection will never be satisfied.

In previous eras, women stayed in difficult marriages because of economic and social pressures. For Christian women, the stigma of divorce and the desire to honor their vows made before God kept many marriages intact. Today, however, our culture bombards us with messages that we deserve someone who fulfills our dreams and that a marriage should be measured by how it makes us feel.

If we're not happy, if our spouse isn't romantic, exciting, successful, or sensitive to our needs and desires, the inner pressure to give up on our marriage can be all-consuming. This pressure is particularly strong if our girlfriends or well-meaning relatives empathize or suggest we deserve better.

> Divorce is a serious matter in God's eyes.
> He meant marriage to knit two people together for
> life in a commitment to each other's well-being.

Like most Christians, I knew divorce was not God's way to solve my problems or soothe my pain. Reading relevant Scriptures made that clear, even to my spiritually immature mind.

Divorce is a serious matter in God's eyes. He meant marriage to knit two people together for life in a commitment to each other's well-being. He also meant marriage to mirror the steadfast, faithful love of Christ for His bride, the church (Ephesians 5:25-33).

Speaking through the prophet Malachi, God made it clear He would not bless His people despite their tears and pleas for His favor. Why? Because they had deliberately broken faith with the wives of their youth and divorced them, which God hated (Malachi 2:13-16).

Jesus also spoke about marriage and divorce, telling His disciples that divorce, except for marital unfaithfulness, was wrong. Asked why Moses granted divorce decrees to the Israelites, Jesus responded, God permitted it "because your hearts were hard" (Matthew 19:8-9).

But What If...?

Though God's ideal is for a man and woman to grow old together, this isn't always possible. There are times when divorce is biblical. And there are times when divorce is the healthiest and safest choice for a woman and her children.

Jill and Barney were married for twenty-one years and had four children. "My husband was extremely controlling, not wanting me to talk to friends on the phone," said Jill, quietly sharing the nightmare she lived through. "He was financially reckless and wouldn't allow us to buy necessities. I worked most of the time, even when I was ill, in order to buy food and clothes. He belittled and criticized me daily, beat me up four times, and was sexually unfaithful.

"I wanted my marriage to last," continued Jill, "and read every Christian book on marriage I could find. I went to seminars. I fasted. I prayed. I cried myself to sleep every night for years because I longed for a loving relationship. When my fourth child turned two, I discovered she was being molested by her father. That was the end of tolerating his behavior. We separated immediately and finally divorced."

> Because this book is not intended to provide counsel for deeply troubled marriages, let me encourage you to get help if your relationship is dangerous or destructive.

Because this book is not intended to provide counsel for deeply troubled marriages, let me encourage you to get help if your relationship is dangerous or destructive. Seek guidance from your pastor or a mature Christian counselor. Help is available. You are not alone. You belong to the God of all compassion who does not ask women to suffer abuse or to allow their children to be abused (2 Corinthians 1:3-5; Isaiah 43:2-7; Mark 9:42).

God cares about you and desires that you be treated with dignity and love. This is His intention for marriage.

Divorce and Guilt

If you have divorced, believe that God does not want you wallowing in what cannot be undone. Whether you or your former husband left your marriage, divorce is not an unpardonable sin. You might have been sinned against, or perhaps you failed to live up to God's holy standard yourself. Regardless of the circumstances, God's Word assures us, "If we confess our sins, he is faithful and just and will forgive us our sins and purify us from all unrighteousness" (1 John 1:9).

In spite of this conscience-cleansing promise, you might still be carrying around a backpack of guilt and shame. If you are, let me encourage you to bring it to God. You might want to cup your hands, hold them up, and give your pain and shame to your loving Father. Then accept by faith that you do not need to stay stuck in the past.

Listen to what the apostle Paul says: "One thing I do: Forgetting what is behind and straining toward what is ahead, I press on toward the goal to win the prize for which God has called me heavenward in Christ Jesus" (Philippians 3:13-14). Did you hear that? He is saying, "Forget the past. Don't dwell on it. Put it out of your mind. It is dealt with. Press on toward all God has for you."

Take a moment and reflect on the healing and hope contained in these Scriptures. What is God saying to you? How will you respond?

Should I? Or Shouldn't I?

Studies show that women file for divorce more often than men.[3] Perhaps it's because we believe that another man or a fresh marriage will bring the happiness we long for. But this assumption that we'll be happier married to someone else needs to be examined in the light of statistics. Second marriages can be successful, but they also have a higher divorce rate than first marriages.

Here are some other popular "Divorce Myths."

Divorce Myth: When the home is full of conflict, children are better off if the parents divorce.

Fact: Conflict does have a negative effect on children. So does getting a divorce. Research shows "only children in very high-conflict homes benefit from the removal of conflict that divorce may bring. In lower-conflict marriages that end in divorce—perhaps as many as two-thirds of the divorces were of this type—the situation of the children was made much worse following a divorce. Based on the findings of this study, therefore, except in the minority of high-conflict marriages, it is better for the children if their parents stay together and work out their problems than if they divorce."[4]

Divorce Myth: Children might be affected by divorce, but they recover quickly. Divorce doesn't have long-term impact.

Fact: Divorce does affect children both in the near and long term.[5] Research by Dr. Robert Hughes, associate professor and extension specialist in the Department of Human Development and Family Science at Ohio State University, found that children of divorce are more likely to have academic problems and experience difficulty in getting along with siblings, peers, and their parents. Boys tend to be more aggressive, and girls struggle with depression.[6]

Divorce Myth: Children of divorced parents will be more careful about getting married and be more determined to avoid divorce.

Fact: Children of divorce experience the breakup of their marriages more often than those from intact families. "A major reason for this, according to a recent study, is that children learn about marital commitment or permanence by observing their parents. In the children of divorce, the sense of commitment to a lifelong marriage has been undermined."[7]

Divorce Myth: Going through times of unhappiness is a predictor the marriage will ultimately fail.

Fact: Going through times of unhappiness occurs in all marriages. Recent research showed three-fifths of couples who once rated their marriages as unhappy now describe them as either "very happy" or "quite happy."[8]

What Is My Part in Building Our Marriage?

Writing about marital struggles, Gary Thomas states the obvious: "Most of those who leave marriage and break its sacred history do so precisely because it is tough. Few people leave a marriage because it's too easy!" He then states some hard truths that many of us don't want to hear. "This tendency to avoid difficulty is a grave spiritual failing that can and often does keep us in Christian infancy. The great spiritual writers warned that this life is difficult and that we should use the difficulty to be built up in our character."[9] Ouch!

Invite God to Change You

In our day of easy Christianity, staying in a difficult relationship and viewing it as an opportunity to develop maturity is rarely considered. Nor is the next step: committing to stay in a marriage out of obedience to the Lord, trusting He will give the grace and wisdom needed to follow Him.

> In our day of easy Christianity, staying in a difficult relationship and viewing it as an opportunity to develop maturity is rarely considered.

When I wrestled with whether to stay or leave, I didn't realize that God intended to use my misery to grow me up. He saw what was possible, even though I didn't. This is how God works. He sees what He can accomplish in our lives and then invites us to cooperate with His plans.

After appearing to Moses in the burning bush, God said, "You are my man to lead the Israelites out of Egypt" (Exodus 3:7-10, Poppy's paraphrase). Moses thought he was a failure and couldn't imagine God had the power to use him. Gideon couldn't see what God intended to make of him, either. He was a nobody in his own eyes with no potential to be different. But God knew better (Judges 6:11-16). And when God called Jeremiah to be His prophet, Jeremiah's response was, "I don't have it in me. I can't be someone I'm not" (Jeremiah 1:4-19, Poppy's paraphrase).

The Bible is full of people like you and me who never imagined they could be so profoundly transformed by God's Spirit. God redirected their characters, priorities, and life focus, and they became someone they never could have been without His power.

By inviting God to show us what He sees in our hearts, our words, and our deeds, we have the same opportunity for change as those who have walked with God through the ages. And when we take the next step, acknowledging what He reveals and asking Him to work in us, we are on our way to experiencing His transforming power.

Have you already sensed God speaking to you about some area that needs His touch? Even if you struggle with several issues, try not to feel overwhelmed. Instead, choose one of these to pray about daily and then watch how God responds. As a reminder of your request, take a moment to write a short prayer that expresses your heart.

_____

_____

_____

_____

Choose to Grow—Don't Give Up

Divorce does not have to be the inevitable response to shattered dreams. Instead, God whispers to every woman who loves Him but struggles to one degree or another with the man she chose to marry, *Don't give up, My child. Grow!*

By drawing closer to Him for whatever we might need—comfort, strength to persevere, self-control, or love, we experience His presence in depths we never imagined. Through our struggles, He becomes more precious, the very source of our strength. The outcome? You will know God in a way you never would have had you married someone just like you!

May I Pray for You?

Heavenly Father, You are the God of all compassion who comforts us in all our troubles. Please comfort Your daughter now and fill her with Your peace. Transform her with Your power. Equip her with everything good for doing Your will, and work in her what is pleasing to You. Amen.

(ADAPTED FROM 2 CORINTHIANS 1:3-4; HEBREWS 13:20-21)

Facing Crossroads—Making Choices

*This is what the L*ORD *says:*
Stand at the crossroads and look.

JEREMIAH 6:16

L ord, please show me a way out," I pleaded daily while wiping down oatmeal-splattered walls, changing my toddler's diapers, and doing laundry. Fixated on my misery, I thought of little else. It never occurred to me that I was standing at a crossroads, a major decision point. Or that I should look down the road and consider what might happen if I got what I prayed for. I just wanted out. But something restrained me. Jesus' words, "If you love me, keep my commands" gripped my heart (John 14:15).

> I just wanted out. But something restrained
> me. Jesus' words, "If you love me, keep my
> commands" gripped my heart (John 14:15).

I did love the Lord and knew He loved me even with all my failings, but to obey Him meant staying in an unhappy marriage. I wrestled with the truth that leaving meant turning away from what He had clearly revealed. Incompatibility and seemingly irreconcilable differences were not biblical grounds for divorce.

Much as I wanted to run back to Africa or England and start again, I couldn't do it. Instead, unable to defy what I knew in my heart was

27

God's will, I accepted my fate. I would be unhappy the rest of my life. *Nothing will ever change*, I told myself. *Not even God can make us happy with each other.*

Nothing will ever change, I told myself. Not even God can make us happy with each other.

Shortly after I reluctantly committed to stay, Jim and I attended a party at a friend's home where we met a former pastor and his wife. Drawn by their gentle manner, I immediately wondered if they could help me figure out how to make the best of a painful situation. I got their phone number, called the next morning, and invited them over that evening. Jim would not be with us because he was on call all night at the hospital.

When I greeted them at the front door, I noticed the pastor had brought his Bible. My heart surged with hope.

They listened quietly as I poured out my hurt and misery. After I finished, the pastor asked, "Poppy, do you think God can change Jim and your situation?"

I shook my head, tears streaming down my cheeks. "No. I don't think it's possible."

They prayed for me and for our marriage, then left. But God had planted a new thought.

Was it possible? Could He really change Jim?

The possibility that He also wanted to change me hadn't yet crossed my mind, and the pastor and his wife were too polite to suggest it.

A Changed Focus

In his book, *The Source of My Strength*, Pastor Charles Stanley says, "I came to adulthood with a heavy load of emotional baggage—little self-esteem, lots of insecurities, a life-long experience of loneliness."[1]

For many years, I didn't realize that much of the pain and conflict in my marriage were rooted in similar emotional baggage. I wanted to feel loved, to delight in belonging to the intelligent and capable man

I married, but whenever we clashed, my hopes sank. Reacting out of growing despair, I responded like a thwarted toddler.

Focused constantly on *my* pain, *my* unhappiness, and *my* inability to change Jim, there was little room to hear God's voice. I had committed to stay in my marriage but had no idea how to improve our relationship.

> Focused constantly on *my* pain,
> *my* unhappiness, and *my* inability to change Jim,
> there was little room to hear God's voice.

Like Pastor Stanley, I didn't understand "how God's transforming grace works in a person's life."[2] But I desperately wanted to. The emotional toll of ping-ponging between despair and anger plus my ugly moods and explosive outbursts finally drove me to my knees. I couldn't go on trapped in my emotions. Sobbing, I prayed, "God, please change me. I hate who I have become. Help me be who You want me to be. Show me how to be different."

> You, LORD, hear the desire of the afflicted;
>   you encourage them, and you listen to their cry.
>   (Psalm 10:17)

In response to my cries, God began to change my focus—from me and my pain, to Him and His purposes for my life. I wanted to know Him, please Him, and be like Him. That's still my deepest desire.

A Changed Direction

When Jim finished his specialty training, we again faced a crossroads. Where would we settle? The outcome of this decision was to affect not just his career, but more importantly, our marriage.

After we moved to Oregon with our three-year-old daughter and three-month-old son, Jim began his medical practice. But God had a new direction for me as well.

Knowing I couldn't cope any longer with the rigid lifestyle of Jim's background, we began searching for a new church. We both understood that if our marriage was to survive, we needed to find something very different, a place where we could grow personally and as a couple.

After five years of longing for a spiritually nurturing environment, God now abundantly provided. We joined a small group of Christians who loved Christ passionately and embraced us warmly. People invited us to their homes for meals. Older ladies offered to watch our little ones in the nursery so I could enjoy the services. We made friends, participated in a home Bible study, and witnessed how ordinary men and women lived out a joy-filled faith.

Not long after we started attending the church, an elder's wife asked if I would like to visit her Bible study, assuring me it had excellent child care. I immediately said yes. The next week I walked into a Bible Study Fellowship class.

For the following five years, I devoured the lessons. Filling all the white space on the question pages, I couldn't write what I was learning fast enough. And nearly every week, the Holy Spirit lovingly spoke through the challenging teaching.

Reading the weekly notes reinforced what God was showing me about my attitudes, behavior, thoughts, and words. The comment, "The world calls children a burden, but God calls them a blessing," sent me to my knees in tears of repentance. God had put me in the right place to prune and purify my heart. And as I grew in my knowledge and desire for Him, He patiently continued the inner work I so desperately needed.

To my amazement, God had something planned for my life I would never have imagined. Now in my early thirties, and still far from being transformed into a sweet, compliant, adoring wife, I was asked to become the teaching leader of my class. Over three hundred women attended each week. Using the Bible and other resources, I would be responsible to lecture on the chapters we were studying.

Jim had seen many positive changes in me over the previous five years and enthusiastically encouraged me to accept. Clearly, he hoped the changes would continue. He began calling me "The Big Enchilada," which made me both blush with embarrassment and laugh out loud.

Even though I felt inadequate biblically and in every other way, I sensed God had opened this door to serve Him. I cared passionately that other women who were mired in hopelessness, needed healing, and longed for a new beginning would experience the reality of a God who transforms the most unlikely people.

Years later, having taught women around the world and listened to their struggles, I am awed at the privilege God has given to share some of what I've learned. Whether through speaking and writing or listening and praying privately with women, I delight in seeing the Lord encourage others through the experiences He has allowed in my life.

Fresh insights and aha moments still happen in our marriage, but now they produce more laughter than tears, acceptance instead of instant anger, and most of the time, a healthy tolerance of our differences. (Though I must confess, at times I still wonder why Jim reasons the way he does.)

> God wants to work in your heart,
> your thinking, and your emotions, bringing you to
> a new level of maturity and Christ-likeness.

As you read through this book, I pray that my personal journey will encourage you to hear God's answers for your life. God wants to work in your heart, your thinking, and your emotions, bringing you to a new level of maturity and Christ-likeness. And your marriage, like mine, is the perfect environment for this to happen.

Standing at Life's Crossroads

The decision to stay in my marriage was life-changing. But I soon faced other crossroads.

The next major one was my attitude. When Jim upset me, I had to decide: Would I stay bitter and angry, slinging out sarcastic barbs, or would I cry out to God to help me zip my lips and change my heart? As the Holy Spirit progressively showed me my inner junk, there were more choices: Would I yield and follow, or resent and resist?

Then God dealt with my expectations, or rather my lack of them. Did I believe that He could change my marriage for the better? Did I believe He could restore my love? Or that He could remove my critical spirit, replacing it with a positive, expectant attitude?

How I chose to respond at these crossroads of my soul determined who I became and the direction of my life. They also affected Jim, and how we related to each other.

Speaking to His people through the prophet Jeremiah, God urged them to recognize where they stood. Israel's continuous worship of idols and disobedience to God's laws had brought them to the brink of exile and enslavement. But there was still time to turn back in repentance. In His mercy, God pleaded with them:

> Stand at the crossroads and look;
>   ask for the ancient paths,
> ask where the good way is, and walk in it,
>   and you will find rest for your souls.
>   (Jeremiah 6:16)

When facing your own crossroads, God says the same thing. *Stand. Look. Ask. Walk.* When you do, He promises you will find rest—inner peace, emotional nourishment, and expectant hope.

With our goal to become women and wives whose lives honor the One who died for us, let's look more closely at this verse. How can these four principles help us make inward and outward choices that are God-pleasing and life-giving?

Stand

When we're in the grip of frustration or emotional pain, standing still can be the hardest principle to follow. Often we're tempted to just do something, anything, simply to find relief from our surging emotions.

When we're in the grip of frustration or emotional pain,
standing still can be the hardest principle to follow.

In His wisdom and concern for us, God first speaks one vital word: *Stand.* In other words, wait. Slow down. Resist the urge to move forward before you have prayed and received His perspective and insight on your situation. When you don't, you can make decisions you soon regret.

The book of Proverbs warns, "The simple believe anything, but the prudent give thought to their steps" (14:15). Unfortunately, instead of standing and thinking carefully about marriage, Christy believed her fiancé's lies and acted on her emotions.

"My parents strongly objected to my relationship with Brad," Christy admitted, "but I wouldn't listen to them. When I met Brad he was recently divorced, but he convinced me it was his first wife's fault. She was demanding and selfish and made his life a misery. Naturally, I felt sorry for him.

"We had only been married a few weeks when Brad started yelling at me if I didn't do what he wanted. He also took off whenever his friends called, leaving me behind. I began to see why his first marriage failed and that it probably wasn't all his wife's fault. I just wish I hadn't rushed into marriage with someone I hardly knew just because I was physically attracted to him."

Many women do rush down the aisle before they've looked carefully at who they are committing themselves to before God. Perhaps you did. And now you're standing at a crossroads.

Is the Holy Spirit cautioning you about a decision you're considering? Perhaps an urge to leave a marriage you rushed into?

Is the Holy Spirit cautioning you about a decision you're considering? Perhaps an urge to leave a marriage you rushed into? Is He trying to get your attention about words, attitudes, or certain behaviors that are undermining your relationship? Take all the time necessary to stand, think carefully about your situation, and seek out His wisdom.

Look

To look is to take more than a quick glance. God wants us to pay attention, be discerning, and wait for His leading. Here are questions to consider as you look:

- How should you handle this situation or relationship in light of God's character and how He has called you to live?

- What are the possible short-term and long-term consequences for you and for others who might be affected?

- If you take this path, does it fit with the overall direction of your life? Is it consistent with your claim to be a follower of Jesus?

- Will this decision lead you, or others who look to you, to a weaker or stronger relationship with God? Will it increase or undermine your faith?

Ask

God says "ask for the ancient paths," the ways He laid out for you to live, choosing what is good, life-giving, and pleasing to Him. Here are some questions to prayerfully ask:

- Which path leads me back to You?

- Which path leads to healing between my husband and me?

- Which path leads to changes needed in me?

- Which path leads me in Your direction for my life?

As you search for God's answers, let me encourage you to do three things:

- *Get into the Bible.* Saturate your mind with its wisdom. Read through Proverbs, the Epistles, and the book of James. Use a modern translation that's easy to read and understand. Join a Bible study or do one on your own. (If you're not sure what Bible study resources would be most helpful, get advice from your pastoral staff or local Christian bookstore.) The more you know what God says about building a good marriage, the greater your chances of having one.

- *Pray.* Pray about what you have read. Ask God to bring it to mind when you need it. Listen to what the Holy Spirit whispers in your heart and act on what you hear.

- *Spend regular time with a spiritual mentor.* Find a God-centered person and ask to meet with them for support and direction, especially as you face difficult issues.

Walk

Going God's way is not always easy, but it comes with a divine promise: You will find rest for your soul.

In my book, *I'm Too Human to Be Like Jesus: Spiritual Growth for the Not-So-Perfect Woman,*[3] I describe many of the struggles I encountered bouncing between wanting to please the Lord but also wanting things my way. Believe me, as I encourage you to listen to the Holy Spirit and allow Him to change you, I know firsthand how hard the process is.

On my knees one morning, I tearfully protested to God. "It's not fair. Why should I do what Jim wants? Why am I supposed to please him? I don't want to."

I sensed the Lord breaking into my list of complaints and asking me, *Poppy, do you love Me? Will you do this for Me?*

"You know I love You, Lord, but it just isn't fair. Why can't I do what I want?"

I heard His voice in my heart a second time. *Poppy, do you love Me? Will you do this for Me?*

Again, I protested. "Lord, I do love You, but why do I have to give in?"

Finally, I sensed the Lord speaking a third time, asking the same question: Would I yield my will and my preference to Jim, because I loved Jesus above having my own way?

There was nothing more to say.

I did yield, and years later that particular difference between us doesn't matter anymore. I now happily do what once caused a rift between us, and Jim never says a word about it.

God's goal for us is transformation into the likeness of Jesus (Romans 8:29). That's not some abstract super-spiritual ideal that has no bearing on our lives and choices. God has a purpose in mind: to create multitudes of "little Christs" who display His character and reveal to the world the reality of a living God. Yielding to what God asks us to do, even if we don't like it, is a vital step toward establishing Him as Lord of our lives. It is how we grow closer to Him and how He makes us into women He can bless and use to bless others.

Throughout the Gospels, Jesus' words give us a picture of what transformation looks like and how it can be seen in our marriages. John 5:30 says, "I seek not to please myself but him who sent me." I'm still working on that characteristic of Christ-likeness and probably will be until my dying day!

What about you? Are you facing a crossroads in your marriage right now? Perhaps over a conflict you feel you must win? Or maybe a temptation you're fighting? Maybe you're wrestling with an issue that involves yielding your will to God. Your struggles might be quite different from the ones that challenged me, but what you decide affects the direction of your life and the quality of your marriage. Your decisions also reveal your heart—whether it is being shaped by Him or ruled by your own will.

What Is My Part in Building Our Marriage?

As you explore how to grow as a follower of Jesus and seek to understand the man you married, let me ask you some challenging but necessary questions:

- Are you willing to look into your own heart?
- Are you willing to look honestly at your contribution to your marriage?
- Are you willing to look at your relationship with God?

We know that the Holy Spirit wants to work in us wherever He sees change is needed. From my experience, I also know that this process is often a two-steps-forward, one-step-back journey. But be encouraged.

Gradually, change does happen—and you might even hear these wonderful words that a friend once said to me: "You are really different." Of course, even more wonderful will be hearing Jesus say (I hope), "Well done, Poppy Smith. You loved Me. You listened to Me. And even though you squirmed a lot, you allowed Me to change you."

That admittedly imaginary scene is my longing for you as well. Is it yours? If so, why not begin moving toward that glorious day by praying for God to speak to you as you mull over the following Scriptures and questions. To preserve what comes to your mind, grab a notebook or journal and record your responses.

- *Look into your heart*: "The fruit of the Spirit is love, joy, peace, forbearance, kindness, goodness, faithfulness, gentleness and self-control" (Galatians 5:22-23).

- *Take inventory*: Which fruit do you see in your heart toward your spouse? Which needs nurturing?

- *Look at your marriage*: Jesus said, "Seek first his kingdom and his righteousness" (Matthew 6:33).

- *Take inventory*: What are you seeking first? How are God's values and priorities influencing how you view your marriage?

- *Look at your relationship with God*: Paul calls every Christian to "make it our goal to please him" (2 Corinthians 5:9).

- *Take inventory*: What are your goals as a Christian for your marriage? What do you sense the Lord is saying to you today?

Believe God Is for You

God wants to bless and encourage you in your walk with Him. He promises:

> "I will lead the blind by ways they have not known,
> along unfamiliar paths I will guide them;
> I will turn the darkness into light before them
> and make the rough places smooth.
> These are the things I will do;

I will not forsake them."
(Isaiah 42:16)

As you ask God to help you work on building a marriage that is as happy as possible, here are some more promises that affirm God is for you:

- *Do you need emotional strength to persevere?* Turn to Jesus who promised: "Come to me, all you who are weary and burdened, and I will give you rest" (Matthew 11:28).

- *Do you wonder how to handle a difficult situation?* Act on James's words: "If any of you lacks wisdom, you should ask God" (James 1:5).

- *Do you need comfort for a hurting heart?* Cling to Jesus' words: "Do not let your hearts be troubled. You believe in God; believe also in me" (John 14:1).

- *Do you long for encouragement?* Embrace this special invitation: "Let us then approach God's throne of grace with confidence, so that we may receive mercy and find grace to help us in our time of need" (Hebrews 4:16).

Prepare for Progress

In addition to the many hope-filled promises God sprinkles like jewels throughout Scripture, His Word also provides practical principles for a healthy marriage. When applied, these principles not only can change us, they can change how we get along with our husbands.

Before change can happen, however, you need to identify what situations keep cropping up to create problems between you. Any issue that repeatedly sets you at odds with each other needs a new approach. Once you've pinpointed one of these, start praying for wisdom. Ask God how He wants you to respond differently. And ask yourself: What other choices am I willing to make in these situations? When will I begin to intentionally follow through with new choices?

The apostle Paul describes the exciting process behind the spiritual and practical changes that happen in the life of a Christian. He says that God is behind our desire, prompting us to hunger to be different and providing the power we need for this to happen. "It is God who works in you to will and to act in order to fulfill his good purpose" (Philippians 2:13).

Our desire and willingness to change involves both *us and God*. God doesn't wave a magic wand and miraculously change us—at least, not usually! Transformation happens through a combination of His Spirit prompting us to make different choices and our response, "Yes, Lord. I will do what pleases You."

When God is at work in us, we have the power to act differently. We don't have to respond to old triggers and negative habits. And every time we choose God's way of handling difficult situations, we accept His invitation to grow.

Are you sensing God at work in you, drawing you to hunger for change? If so, begin with applying the following nine practical principles that are a taste of what's to come in the rest of this book.

But be warned. These principles are not necessarily easy to practice. I know, because I learned them all the hard way. Still, I encourage you to ask yourself, "How might this particular principle apply in my situation? Am I willing to take a risk and try this today? Will I trust that God is for me and promises His blessing when I do what pleases Him?

1. Accept you may never agree on some issues.

Your romantic ideal of living in perfect harmony needs to be traded in for reality. Some things that bother you might never change. Certain needs, desires, and dreams you expected from marriage might never be met in that relationship. What will your focus be now? How will you work positively with what you *do* have?

2. Compromise and be willing to flex.

Whether it's where to plant flowers, where to celebrate Christmas, or where to spend your bonus, stubbornly refusing to compromise leads to power-fights and resentful feelings. Look for win-win solutions. Remember your goal is to have a positive relationship, not conquer an enemy.

3. Compensate with healthy female friendships.

This is vital if your need for someone to chat with is going nowhere at home. I know the ideal spouse is a combination of best friend, closest companion, confidante, supporter, and adviser. If you have this, praise God. If not, find some friends who can help supply what you're missing. Lunch is cheaper than therapy.

4. Develop a closer relationship with God.

Tell the Lord exactly how you're feeling. The truth is He knows anyway. Being honest with yourself and with God is healthy. Read and memorize Scriptures that speak of God as your tender Shepherd. Remind yourself that He is the One who unfailingly loves you, even when you can't see how this could be true. Your struggles can produce a closeness to the Lord for which you will eventually thank Him.

5. Communicate with love and honesty.

Your husband is not a mind reader. How is he to know you have a migraine, the kids have been wild, and your mother is upset with you unless you tell him? If you have a need, say so nicely and clearly. Ask him if he can help instead of assuming that if he loved you he would know what to do. Most likely he doesn't, so speak up and show appreciation for whatever he does.

6. Concentrate on the positive.

Check out the list in Philippians 4:8. Record what is praiseworthy, true, good, and positive about your husband. Ask God to show you other traits and behaviors that you appreciate. Then verbalize them to your spouse in a way that doesn't embarrass him.

7. Consider and learn from past conflicts.

Think about previous fights and disagreements. What did you learn about yourself and your husband? How could you have handled things differently? Ask God to show you what words inflame and what words soothe. Where could you start putting this insight into practice?

8. Commit yourself to speaking well of him.

Your husband is not a jerk. He's not a loser. He doesn't deserve to be labeled a failure. Whatever his faults, whether you're speaking about him to others inside the family or out, ask God to set a guard over your mouth. You are giving a picture to others of the man you married, possibly the father of your children. He is a man God desires to reach and powerfully change. So ask yourself: Is what I'm tempted to say pleasing to the Lord? Does it contribute to the relationship I long for?

9. PUT YOUR HOPE IN GOD.

You and your husband can do many little things to improve your relationship, but no quick fixes exist when you're married to someone who is not like you. Change doesn't happen quickly or easily. But one day, to your utter amazement, you might notice how you handled an irritating situation with maturity and wisdom. Instead of pouting or withdrawing, you spoke with kindness and love, and the shock makes you clap your hands, shout "Praise God," and do a little jig around your kitchen. (At least, that's how I've reacted from time to time.)

Dream of that day, my friend. With God, nothing is impossible. You and that baffling, frustrating, and occasionally infuriating man you married can indeed make it.

May I Pray for You?

Father, fill Your daughter with all joy and peace as she trusts in You so that she may overflow with hope by the power of the Holy Spirit. Give her endurance, encouragement, and a spirit of unity with her husband as she follows You, so that with one heart and mouth they may both give You the glory. Amen.

(ADAPTED FROM ROMANS 15:5-6,13)

PART 2

He's Not Like Me Because...

Three

He's Not My Clone!

Accept one another, then, just as Christ accepted
you, in order to bring praise to God.

ROMANS 15:7

Mmm, it smells like French perfume," Jim teased as we drove past a hog barn on a humid August day in Iowa. Raised on a dairy farm, my husband took barnyard smells in stride. They made me gag.

As a love-struck bride, I assumed my husband was normal. The definition of "normal" being me, of course. Therefore, I expected Jim would react to everything the same way I did.

Stumbling through the first months and years of marriage, however, it became increasingly clear that our ideas of normal didn't match. I had not found my clone. I wanted to go out on Sunday afternoons. Jim wanted to nap. I wanted to replace the ugly, brown, Early American wallpaper in our first home. Jim thought there was nothing wrong with it.

Instead of "two hearts beating as one," our two hearts, minds, and wills beat individually. And each wondered what was wrong with the other.

Instead of "two hearts beating as one," our two
hearts, minds, and wills beat individually. And each
wondered what was wrong with the other.

In teaching about different personality types, speaker and author Florence Littauer describes the moment she first realized she had not married her clone. While she was eating a bunch of sweet, purple grapes on the balcony of their honeymoon suite, her husband, Fred, came out and watched. After a few moments he said, "You are not eating those grapes properly."

"What's wrong with how I'm eating them?" Florence asked. "I pick one off the stem and pop it in my mouth. How do you think I should do it?"

"With a knife and fork," Fred responded. "That's how I was raised."

Differences Aren't Always Delightful

Some happily married couples describe their differences as complementing and strengthening their relationship. This may not be the case in your situation. The distance between you on many issues may be slowly chinking away at your soul, leaving you frustrated, furious, or tearfully moaning, "Why can't he see things my way?"

One or more of these reactions is especially true if you start out believing you will see eye to eye on most things, process information the same way, and eventually come to the same conclusions. Without realizing it, you assumed you were marrying your clone.

According to the Human Genome Project, cloning is an umbrella term traditionally used by scientists to describe different processes for duplicating biological material.[1] Cloning produces the genetic twin of another organism. But, guess what? It hasn't happened yet at the human level. So much for those fantasies about marrying someone just like yourself.

Chasing Fantasies

Being married doesn't guarantee you won't be attracted to other men or be tempted to daydream about them. If you enjoy someone with a sense of humor, you'll continue to find pleasure in being around good-natured, witty men. Are you drawn to serious-minded or creative types? You'll continue to like talking to men with those qualities. You don't lose part of your personality once you say, "I do."

As a red-blooded woman, however, and especially if you're in a marriage that leaves you emotionally vulnerable, be careful to notice signs of sexual attraction. Looking for ways to be with one man in particular, spending alone time together, and thinking about him when you're apart are all red flags that God wants you to take seriously.

Beyond enjoying innocent friendships, however, you might still dream that somewhere in this world your clone exists (and is longing to find you as much as you want to find him). As grown women we have to face reality: no such man is out there. We also have to face the fact that the men we didn't marry, the ones who got away or who we rejected, were not our clones either.

Marilyn, a married, fiftysomething accountant, discovered this after coming dangerously close to starting an affair with her old high-school sweetheart. Frustrated with her quiet, calm, and somewhat boring husband, Marilyn often fantasized about how much fun she had with Jason decades before. She decided to look him up on the Internet. Once she discovered his email address, the temptation to contact him obsessed her.

A few days later, heart pounding, Marilyn carefully crafted a casual email asking Jason how he and his family were and if he would be attending their high-school reunion. Then she hit Send.

As a wife and active Christian, Marilyn fought her sense of guilt by rationalizing that there was nothing wrong in contacting Jason. Probably both of them would be at the reunion, so it was only natural to connect after all these years and arrange a meeting.

Jason responded immediately, excited to be back in touch. At the reunion, he lost no time suggesting they make excuses to their spouses and plan a weekend together. Marilyn was thrilled at the idea. All her old feelings for Jason came surging back. Using their work addresses, they exchanged passionate letters as they made plans for their forbidden weekend.

Then God stepped in. Shortly before finalizing her plans, Marilyn attended a women's retreat. "The speaker said fantasizing about old boyfriends was not honoring to God," Marilyn recounted as we discussed her spiritual journey. "She told us how God had convicted her of this sin many years before, and that if we wanted Jesus to be Lord of our lives, He had to be Lord of our minds also. I was so angry that I left the auditorium, but I knew that my plans were not okay with God no matter how hard I tried to convince myself."

Face-to-face with how she had almost thrown away the respect of her daughters and the love of a faithful husband, Marilyn recognized her delusion. In her fantasies, she and Jason were clones, meant to be together. They found each other attractive, exciting. Their personalities clicked. They laughed at the same things. Surely any reasonable person could see they would be happier together than with their spouses. Could it be wrong to pursue being with someone you found so compatible?

Marilyn's story may sound like a soap opera, but fantasizing about an ideal relationship with someone other than your husband isn't unusual. It is a common response to marital frustration. The greater your frustration, the more likely you are to evaluate whether you want to stay in your marriage or consider other choices.

To begin your journey toward a better relationship, you need to do two things. First, choose to give up dreaming about other men and the fantasy that somewhere out there your clone exists. Second, throw out your unrealistic expectations of marriage and accept what is real:

- You and your spouse are inevitably different.
- You are two unique people with your own set of convictions, viewpoints, likes, and dislikes.
- You look at issues differently for good reason: you were shaped by different home environments, cultural expectations, religious backgrounds, educational experiences, and life lessons.
- You don't have to share identical views to make your marriage work.
- A perfect spouse does not exist.

I wish I had understood these facts in those early years, but it never occurred to me at that time to try to uncover why Jim and I differed on so many issues. Once I started thinking about our backgrounds, however, I saw many reasons why we clashed.

To help you learn more about yourself and your husband, try this quick quiz that covers a variety of situations found in most marriages. Check off where you usually have the same response, are somewhat similar, or completely opposite. At the end, add up your scores for each category. Your answers will provide a glimpse into where you differ and where you are alike. We'll look at possible reasons for this in the rest of the chapter.

I Respond—He Responds

Personality: When an exciting event happens, such as one of us receives a promotion or bonus, my response is _____

_____

His response: ❑ Same ❑ Similar ❑ Opposite

Chores: When a task is overdue, perhaps weeding the flowerbeds or paying bills, my usual response is _____

_____

His response: ❑ Same ❑ Similar ❑ Opposite

Family: When either of our families need something, maybe help getting a job done, my usual response is _____

_____

His response: ❑ Same ❑ Similar ❑ Opposite

Spending: When I see an item I want to buy, say cute shoes, even if money is tight, my usual response is _____

_____

When he wants to buy something, his response is:

                          ❑ Same ❑ Similar ❑ Opposite

Expressing Pain: When I cut my finger or stub my toe, my usual response is _____

When in pain, his response is: ❑ Same   ❑ Similar   ❑ Opposite

Feelings: When my feelings are hurt, my usual response is _____
_____

When he feels hurt, his response is: ❑ Same   ❑ Similar   ❑ Opposite

Goal Setting: When we discuss future plans, perhaps where to go on vacation or when to visit our parents, my usual response is _____
_____

His response: ❑ Same   ❑ Similar   ❑ Opposite

Stress: When I feel under pressure to meet a deadline or someone's expectations, my usual response is _____
_____

Under pressure, his response is: ❑ Same   ❑ Similar   ❑ Opposite

When Needing Help: When I realize I need help, perhaps to get a job completed or our home ready for company, my usual response is __
_____

His response: ❑ Same   ❑ Similar   ❑ Opposite

Attending Church: When it's time to get ready for church and we're running late, my usual response is _____
_____

His response: ❑ Same   ❑ Similar   ❑ Opposite

Donating Money: When there are appeals for financial donations to meet critical or ongoing needs, my usual response is _____
_____

His response: ❑ Same   ❑ Similar   ❑ Opposite

Different Interests: When we have different ideas on where to spend a free Saturday, my usual response is _____

_____

His response:　　　　　　　　□ Same　□ Similar　□ Opposite

Scoring key: Same = 2 points Similar = 1 point Opposite = 0 points

Totals:　Same _____　　　Similar _____　　Opposite _____

Quite compatible: 18–24

Somewhat compatible: 10–17

Occasionally compatible: 4–9

We have problems: 0–3

Do you differ on other issues? Jot them down here as a reminder to look for helpful suggestions as you read this book:

_____

_____

_____

Why Do We See Things So Differently?

A poster in a woman's locker room advertised a marriage seminar. Printed in bold letters was the question, "What do you and your husband have in common?" Scrawled across it in red ink were the words, "We got married on the same day!"

Are you smiling in agreement with this frustrated, anonymous woman? Even if her answer is funny, are there times when you ask yourself, *Why do we see things so differently? Will we ever learn to accept our differences and begin to understand each other? Is there something I could be doing to bring about positive changes in our relationship?*

Let me assure you, you can discover where some of your differences originate. Although it's not possible to unearth all the contributing factors, here are three possibilities to help you understand why you didn't marry your clone.

You Come from One Culture, He Comes from Another

Culture means having shared experiences, beliefs, and values that shape how you understand the world, interpret events, and behave as an individual and in a group or community. You don't have to be married to someone from another country or ethnicity to experience a cross-cultural marriage. Even if you married the boy next door, you come from different cultures, different homes, different parents, different siblings and relatives. You possibly absorbed different values, were taught different ways to handle your feelings, and different ways to relate to people.

> You don't have to be married to someone from another country or ethnicity to experience a cross-cultural marriage.

The movie *My Big Fat Greek Wedding* is full of the humor and tensions that are part of a cross-cultural marriage. The bride's boisterous, extended Greek family kiss everyone, vehemently express their opinions, delight in dancing, drinking, and taking part in their traditional wedding customs. The groom's parents are reserved, suspicious, unenthusiastic, and completely overwhelmed. Perceived as strange and unfriendly by the bride's relatives, they sit primly in the living room, grimly observing the festivities.

At the wedding reception, the bride's father and mother present the happy couple with the ultimate gift that expresses their bond as a family and culture. They give the bride and groom a deed for their first home—on the same street as theirs. In fact, right next door.

I was raised with two sisters and parents who communicated easily. We talked at the dinner table, while we watched television, and when we went out as a family. Jim's parents, however, tended toward silence. They could sit in the same room or the same car without any conversation, while I chatted away because I was raised that this was the socially polite thing to do.

I couldn't understand why his parents didn't say anything. Feeling rejected and a bit ridiculous, I immediately thought, *They are really strange and unfriendly.* It took me many years to recognize they weren't being rude. They just weren't verbally expressive and felt no compulsion to respond.

How about you? Have you had some puzzling or awkward cross-cultural experiences? Proverbs 15:14 says, "The discerning heart seeks knowledge." Let me encourage you to look back at situations that have confused you. What can you learn from those experiences about your spouse and yourself?

You Come from One Place, He Comes from Another

After living for two years in a small town in Iowa, I couldn't wait to spend a weekend in Chicago. Following hours of dreary driving, my excitement bubbled over when I saw the hazy outline of skyscrapers rising high above the flat landscape.

"Let's go to the Adler Planetarium first," I said, barely stopping for breath. "Then check out the Museum of Science and Industry, and tomorrow we can go shopping and visit the Museum of Contemporary Art. We've got to have Chicago pizza and ride the trolley and walk by Lake Michigan. There's so much to do and it will be such fun. I love cities, don't you, Jim?"

Smiling at my enthusiasm, my former farm-boy husband responded honestly. "No, I don't love cities. I hate them. They are noisy, smelly, crowded, and expensive. I'm glad you're excited about visiting Chicago, but it isn't my idea of where to go for a good time."

Did you know that *where* you were raised can be another reason you're different?

Val Farmer, columnist for *Iowa Farmer Today*, researched the differences between people raised in rural and urban settings. He found that experiences common to people in rural areas, such as relative isolation, being rooted in one place, and having ongoing, lifelong relationships, have a distinct effect on how they view life and what values they hold. Some of these values include maintaining community and family ties, preferring security and predictability over risk and change, and being generally cautious about confiding important and personal matters to other people.[2]

Jim had no interest in city life. He was raised with the quiet, predictable rhythm of life on the farm. He didn't appreciate traffic or crowds, didn't need excitement, and had no desire to spend a weekend rushing from one event to another. But he knew how much I craved the stimulation. Driving back to Iowa on Sunday night, he did admit it wasn't as awful as he had expected. In fact, he had enjoyed himself.

How about you? Could some of your struggles be linked to where you were raised and how that influenced what you now enjoy? Ask God to help you see what's behind your preferences. You'll find it easier to understand and accept one another once you recognize these possible links to the past.

You Speak One Love Language, He Speaks Another

Do you sometimes wonder why you don't *feel* loved by your husband, even if he regularly whispers those three little words? According to Dr. Gary Chapman, author of *The Five Love Languages,* we perceive love in different ways. It's as if we have antenna attached to the top of our heads, trained to pick up the signals that come in on our personal wavelengths.

Based on his extensive counseling practice, Dr. Chapman discovered that our highly sensitive receptors register love in one of five ways:

- *Words of affirmation*—giving compliments, praise, and appreciation
- *Quality time*—paying attention, laying aside your plans to be with the other
- *Receiving gifts*—not necessarily expensive, but thoughtful expressions of love
- *Acts of service*—helping in the home, serving others' needs or desires
- *Physical touch*—giving hugs, pats, physically expressing affection and love

Providing yet more evidence that none of us married our clones, Dr. Chapman found few couples had the same love language.

Growing up with lots of affirmation from my parents, I am thrilled when someone affirms me, whether in person or via a note or email. That's my love language. However, I married a man from a home that didn't practice affirmation or give compliments. Remember, they weren't verbal people. Jim's antenna does receive love, however. It just comes via a wavelength I'm still learning about.

When Jim asked me to take him to the airport and pick him up a few days later, my pragmatic mind jumped into action. "Why don't you just park at the long-term parking lot? That way, I won't have to get up at 4:00 a.m. to take you or drive out there in the dark of night to pick you up." It seemed so reasonable to me.

Frowning at my obvious reluctance to drive him, Jim muttered, "If you cared for me, you'd be willing to do this."

Discovering that acts of service spell L-O-V-E to Jim, I am more careful about suggesting ways to avoid doing what he asks. But I must admit it's hard not to run my alternative solutions past him.

Now that you have uncovered some of the differences between you and your husband and know why they exist, let's move on to the next step. Ask yourself:

- In what areas of my marriage do I want to see changes?
- How could these new insights make a difference in our relationship?
- What steps can I take to apply one of them now?

Take time to think about these three questions. Then let's look at what you can do to increase the happiness factor in your marriage.

What Is My Part in Building Our Marriage?

One of the marks of a Christian is acceptance of others. Romans 15:7 says, "Accept one another, then, just as Christ accepted you, in order to bring praise to God." Given the great diversity between people, both within and outside the church, this basic principle for Christian living challenges our tendency to accept only those who are like us.

Accepting someone doesn't mean you must agree with their ideas or ways of doing things. But it does mean allowing them to be themselves without criticism and judgment.

Let's explore this principle and see how it applies to marriage.

Practicing Acceptance

Barb knew all about trying to change Dave, her husband of thirty years. "Dave's idea of being helpful is to pick up his dish, rinse it off, and leave it on the counter." She laughed as she half-complained to her amused friends over lunch.

"He also eats every scrap of food on his plate even though I've tried telling him it isn't polite. At least, that's how I was brought up. Do you know what he tells me? He says that is how he was raised and he sees no reason to change."

Dave's habits had irritated Barb for years. But from his perspective, there was no harm in what he did, and he felt she was making a fuss about nothing. This left Barb with two choices: Keep fuming and lecturing, or look the other way and accept him as he is.

Perhaps you identify with Barb. Maybe your husband has habits that are difficult for you to live with. But learning to adjust to one another and accepting that we can't have everything our way comes with being married. There is a difference, however, between accepting and adjusting to habits we don't like and ignoring acts of sin.

Adapting to Differences or Accepting Sin?

In her biblically grounded book, *The Emotionally Destructive Relationship,* Christian counselor Leslie Vernick describes some of the ways you can distinguish between a merely annoying habit and sinful behavior that needs attention. She describes a sin-prompted, destructive relationship as showing evidence of abuse: physical, emotional, verbal, or sexual.

Behavior that needs addressing, according to Vernick, is when one spouse deceives the other, lies, hides, pretends, misleads, or twists information. Chronic indifference and neglect toward the feelings and well-being of the other are also sin-prompted behaviors.[3] These are not simply harmless habits your spouse grew up with or adopted. They are not merely ways of behaving that you should accept and ignore. They are destructive patterns God never intended to be part of a healthy marriage.

If you sense you need help sorting through some behaviors that produce pain and confusion in your relationship, don't shrink from finding someone you can talk to in confidence. Your pastor or women's ministry leaders are good places to begin.

You Can Change Only Yourself

No one has the power to change another person's habits or behaviors. You can state your preferences, ask for changes, pout, nag, or lose your temper, but you cannot force another person to change.

Of course, you could threaten certain consequences, but that is hardly the way to build a happier marriage. Your spouse can also ask you to change, but he can't make you—unless he too uses methods that destroy rather than build your relationship.

Changes in how you relate to each other can happen, but it begins with your decision to accept your husband for who he is, quirks and all. Then comes the practical work of looking at what you can do to have a happier marriage. Are you motivated to move forward? If so, let's begin looking at the areas you most want changed.

What Changes Do You Want?

There might be aspects of your marriage that constantly grate on you, or you might be blessed with only a few minor irritants that crop up occasionally. Whatever the degree of your differences, here are some ways to create positive change.

Step One: Think about those areas where your differences create tension. Make a list of them, but don't go overboard. Limit your list to ten items. With this overview in front of you, circle the three you find most stressful.

_____

_____

_____

Step Two: Now list the three areas you circled. Dream a little and ask yourself, *What would it look like if the changes I want actually happened?*

1. _____

2. _____

3. _____

Step Three: When you and your husband clash, there is an emotional toll on both of you and on your relationship. You can't be happy and hostile at the same time, nor can you be intimate and loving toward your husband when you are fuming. For your marriage to improve, you need to be honest about your feelings—with yourself, your husband, and with God. As you look at the three areas listed above, ask yourself:

How do I feel when we clash on these issues? Accused? Rejected? Anxious? Inferior? Weary? Some other emotion?

_____

_____

What have I told my husband about how I feel when we clash? What effect did this have? _____

Now that you have identified the three areas that make the most impact on your happiness, let's look at what *is* in your power to change.

Apply God's Principles

Instead of believing that unless your husband changes all is hopeless, choose to look at your differences with eyes of faith. You are not stuck in an impossible situation. That is a lie from the evil one, who is the god of all discouragement. You *can* see your relationship turn around, and here are six concrete steps to get you started.

1. Seek God's help.

Begin by asking God to help you see your heart. This is ground zero for any transformation. As tough as it is to stop looking at your husband's faults and focus on your own, swallow hard and ask the Holy

Spirit to show you what needs confessing and cleansing. Then act on it. Ask yourself, *Do I focus more on my husband's faults than his good points? Am I wrapped up in judging and criticizing him, letting him know that he has failed to make me happy?*

2. Reject shame.

Don't allow acknowledgement of your faults to become a source of shame. No one is perfect. If we were, we wouldn't need Christ's forgiveness or the Holy Spirit's power in our lives. Determine to be honest with yourself and face your failings, but don't stay stuck in the negative. Tell God what is going on in you and ask for His help.

3. Stop the blame game.

Adam and Eve made choices, but when these resulted in trouble, they were quick to say the other was at fault. Sound familiar? Although blaming your husband when you're frustrated with him is the most natural response, it isn't inevitable. No one forces you to react the way you do. Taking responsibility for how you handle a stressful situation is a power God has given you. Ask Him for the self-control or different perspective needed to change your response.

4. Risk and share your feelings.

Instead of arguing about your differences and trying to assign blame, stop and ask yourself how the situation makes you feel. Try and look beneath generalities such as anger or hurt and identify a feeling that more accurately expresses what is happening in you. Could your reaction be rooted in feeling unloved, scorned, unvalued, or disrespected? Take a risk and be vulnerable. Share with your husband the effect your clashes have on you. This not only helps him know who you are on a deeper level, it also begins to build empathy. When you ask him how he is affected by your differences, you can also develop empathy for him.

5. Change your mental messages.

The words you tell yourself about your spouse inevitably come out of your mouth. We speak what we think, which is why Jesus pointedly stated, "The things that come out of a person's mouth come from the heart, and these defile them" (Matthew 15:18). Our hearts are the source of our ugly attitudes and actions, and in Scripture the heart and mind are often synonymous.

But you are not helpless to change your inner talk. As God's child, you have the Holy Spirit's power available whenever you ask.

A good place to start is by praying for the power to stop being picky and faultfinding. Ask God to give you positive words to replace the negative. You can build loving feelings toward your spouse by choosing to focus on his strengths and remembering all that is good about him. Pray for the ability to do this, practice it daily, and you'll be amazed at the way your mood toward him can change. So will what comes out of your mouth.

6. LOOK FOR MIDDLE GROUND.

Look back at the three most difficult areas you identified. How could you work out a compromise? Is there something your husband would like you to do with him or for him that for you has all the appeal of going to the dentist? Is there something you want him to do with you, but he is just as resistant? How could you meet each other in the middle?

If you feel pressured to always do what your husband wants, or you realize you pressure him to do your bidding, step back from the destructive power play. Suggest instead that you take turns doing what the other wants based on how important the issue is to each of you. This prevents unfair treatment by the one who usually gets their way and avoids resentment for the other.

Remember, you cannot make your husband agree to compromise, but you can demonstrate your willingness to meet him halfway. Creating positive ways to deal with your differences will invariably contribute to your goal: A marriage that is as happy as possible between two people who could never be mistaken for clones.

Choose to Grow

Let me gently repeat what we need to constantly keep in mind. Although we cannot transform our marriages on our own, with God's help we can experience personal transformation. It takes humility—the willingness to see what needs changing in us. It takes dropping our defensiveness and listening to what our spouse is saying by his words or actions, even if we don't like the message. It takes speaking up and refusing to go along with whatever offends the Lord. It takes praying for eyes to see our spouse, especially at the most irritating times, as a man loved by God. And it takes knowing that, with all our own failings, we too are dearly loved and accepted by Him.

May I Pray for You?

O Lord, You have examined my sister's heart and know everything about her. You know when she sits down or stands up. You know her every thought. You know what she is going to say even before she says it. Lord, place Your hand of blessing on my friend. Search her heart, O God, and point out anything in her that offends or grieves You. Teach her how to live in Your power, believing that You are at work in her. Give her eyes to watch with joyful anticipation for the changes You will make in her. Amen.

(ADAPTED FROM PSALM 139)

Four

We Weren't Raised in the Same Home

By wisdom a house is built,
and through understanding it is established.

PROVERBS 24:3

watched in horror as the gravy on my mashed potatoes flowed like a dark-brown river around the green Jell-O salad. *Do they eat dessert along with their main course? Is that why it's all on the same plate?*

Sitting at my in-laws' table for the first time, I realized that the jiggling Jell-O, surrounded by a moat of congealing gravy, vividly illustrated two things: My husband and I were raised in different homes. And clearly, my home was the normal one.

Jim and I both come from a traditional family with a father, mother, and siblings. But our home life had little else in common.

You might have been raised by a stepparent, a single mom, grandparents, or in a foster home. Whatever environment you grew up in, what was modeled and expected of you became your concept of normal. Then you get married and are shocked to discover that your idea of normal does not match your husband's.

> Whatever environment you grew up in, what was modeled and expected of you became your concept of normal.

Eating Jell-O with meat and mashed potatoes jolted me, but my British heritage trained me to always be polite. I knew better than to react visibly or verbally. However, that didn't stop me from thinking this behavior was bizarre.

Check Your Roots

If different eating habits were the only trifling irritants we had to deal with in bonding as a couple, we wouldn't need to explore how our homes have influenced who we are as adults. But the world our parents created for us lingers in our psyche and shapes how we create our own marriage.

When Jim and I declared "I do" and drove off into the sunset for an idyllic honeymoon, I thought we were leaving our families behind and creating a new one. Determined to cleave to my spouse, I never noticed that hitched to our wedding getaway car was a trailer inscribed with the words, "We're still with you!" and signed, "Your Families."

Every one of us steps into marriage with assumptions, expectations, attitudes, and behavior patterns from our upbringing. Like most couples, Jim and I were unaware of this. But we soon found ourselves struggling because of the differences in our backgrounds.

> Every one of us steps into marriage with
> assumptions, expectations, attitudes, and
> behavior patterns from our upbringing.

Some of our differences were minor, like my habit of having two or three flavors of jam or marmalade open at the same time. "Why can't you finish one before opening the other?" Jim asked me once.

"Because one day I might want strawberry jam and the next day I might want orange marmalade. Is that okay?"

Though he still thought I should finish one jar before opening another, my answer seemed to satisfy Jim's logical left-brain thinking.

Other differences were major, like where the dog would live. When we got our first puppy, I discovered that Jim's family always had a dog, but it was kept outside in the barn or a doghouse. In contrast, I held to the proper English perspective: the dog stays inside except when taken out for "walkies." In my home it was understood that a dog's rightful place is by your chair as you read the newspaper.

With strong feelings on both sides about a dog's place, we never did find a win-win solution. Twiga, our golden retriever, stayed outside. I was not happy with Jim's decision, but rather than constantly argue over a belief firmly fixed in his mind, I yielded. I have to admit, it was not easy.

To my delight, years later our two children took sweet revenge when they had their own homes. Their dogs not only live indoors, they also sleep on their owners' beds.

When we don't understand where our different perspectives come from or their amazing power to stick to us like Velcro, it's easy to be hurt, feel unloved, or become irritated and angry. These were often my instinctive reactions.

Like most women, I took our misunderstandings personally. Being the expressive type, I would speak up and then end up bursting into tears of frustration!

Like most women, I took our misunderstandings personally. Being the expressive type, I would speak up and then end up bursting into tears of frustration! Your way of handling these conflicts might be very different from mine. Perhaps you use the silent treatment, sarcasm, or some other style modeled by one of your parents. However we respond, negative interactions slowly drain the life and joy out of our marriages.

Because differences tied to our upbringing can be a significant source of discouragement and emotional pain, we need to look at them, not ignore them. My purpose in this chapter is to help you do that.

One day, after moaning and groaning to God about Jim's unfathomable mind-set, God turned on a megawatt lightbulb in my brain: If you want to understand your husband, look at his background.

If you want to understand your husband, look at his background.

Our clashes over so many issues finally made sense. Learning how Jim was raised and sharing how we did things in my family released much of my anger and frustration. Of course we saw things differently. Why wouldn't we?

According to author and counselor Dr. Roger Hillerstrom, "Unseen factors live in our past. Some are positive, healthy characteristics... Some are stumbling blocks that keep us from experiencing life at its best. Often we have no idea they even exist!"[1]

It goes without saying that some differences come from simply being male or female, having different personalities, and having brains that process on different wavelengths. We'll look at these and other factors in the next chapter.

Your backgrounds might not be as far apart as ours. Nevertheless, understanding the powerful role of your pasts is not the only reason to look back. God wants the insights you've gained to produce positive change. He wants you to learn practical ways to blend your two different but equally valid points of view. This is vital in order to build the kind of marriage you want—one that honors God and is characterized by understanding, acceptance, and compromise. Notice I didn't say *agreement*.

Unpacking Your Trailer

Like unpacking a trailer full of boxes, gaining wisdom and being willing to adapt and change takes work. It also takes opening yourself up to God's help and praying for the love, patience, and positive attitude required to build a good marriage. Remember, He wants to bless your relationship and invites you to "Call to me and I will answer you and tell you great and unsearchable things you do not know" (Jeremiah 33:3). Though this promise is specifically addressed to the prophet Jeremiah, you can be assured that God invites you to call upon Him for understanding. This applies not just to the great mysteries of God; it also applies to your need for insight. Once you begin calling out to Him for wisdom, be sure to start watching for His answers.

To help you begin unpacking your trailer and opening up all those tightly sealed boxes, take a little time to work through the following questions. But don't worry. This look back isn't intended to be a psychological analysis of your family, nor is it meant to point blame at good old Mom and Dad.

Before you dig in, let me encourage you to sit quietly and pray for wisdom. Ask the Holy Spirit to bring to mind anything that would be helpful in understanding how you and your husband relate.

If possible, try to recruit your mate to work through these questions with you. Open up, listen to each other's stories, and learn what shaped your lives. What you discover might surprise you, and if viewed with interest and empathy, can help you both feel more connected and understood.

Look Back—and Learn

Describe and compare your family of origin:

Who raised you? _____

How did your parents handle conflict? _____

_____

How would you describe the general atmosphere in your home? ____

_____

Describe your family lifestyle:

Was your home messy or did everything have its place? _____

_____

Were others welcome in your home or was the focus on "our family"?

_____

What did your parents model regarding faith? _____

_____

Describe your family's expectations:

What was expected of you academically or in other school-related activities? _____

_____

How was discipline and correction carried out? _____

_____

How did your parents show emotional support? Or did you receive damaging messages? _____

_____

What freedom did you have to express your feelings?

_____

List three things you're thankful for concerning your upbringing:

_____

_____

_____

List three negative influences that you have overcome or still wrestle with:

_____

_____

_____

What have you learned about yourself and your spouse from this exercise? Do you better understand now why you clash in certain areas? How can you apply this new knowledge?

_____

_____

Who Does What Task?

On the way to bed one night, I noticed the front door was unlocked.

Turning to Jim, I said, "I wish you would check the doors and windows at night to make sure they're locked. I think it's your job as the man in this house to make sure we're safe."

"We never locked anything on the farm, night or day. No one is going to break in and get you," he responded. "And if they do, I promise I'll protect you. Is that okay?"

No it wasn't. I appreciated Jim's assurance that he'd protect me, but I wanted him to take appropriate action before, not after, we got mugged in our own home. My father always checked the doors and windows at night. I grew up feeling safe because he took his role as protector of the family seriously. Naturally, I assumed all husbands did this.

How did we resolve our different attitudes for thwarting potential burglars or rapists? Knowing Jim doesn't think about locking doors or see that as part of his role as the man of the house, I now check them myself.

Changed Culture—Changed Roles

Assumptions about who should do various tasks are often shaped by how our mom and dad juggled the need to earn an income and run the home. If Dad paid the bills, made the major decisions, and acted as the disciplinarian, that is what you or your spouse might expect of the man's role. If your mom took an equally traditional role and did the shopping, cooking, cleaning, and laundry, then it's likely that's the model you assume is normal.

On the other hand, you might have been raised in a home where both parents brought in the money and tackled tasks together. Or you might have seen your mother, whether single or married, not only working outside the home but also juggling everything else.

We watched and absorbed what was modeled in our home and developed the belief that our family's way was normal.

We watched and absorbed what was modeled in our home and developed the belief that our family's way was normal. As we grow up and get exposed to various other ways of living and dividing the chores, however, we see that there is no one right way. Who does what depends on the individuals involved and what works best for them.

Shared Responsibilities

Data drawn from a survey of fifty thousand couples affirms that with a high percentage of women working outside the home, a marriage where all the responsibilities are shared brings the most satisfaction. After analyzing this extensive study, two characteristics of happy couples stood out. First, both partners were willing to adjust their schedules and preferences to make their lives run more smoothly. Second, both were willing to work toward having an equal relationship.[2]

"Happy couples have a more balanced relationship in terms of *roles* than do unhappy couples," say the authors of *The Couple Checkup*. They also note that although many couples try to dismiss role allocation as trivial, it has a deep influence on the quality of a marriage.[3]

If your assumptions about who should do what creates conflict, here are some questions to consider regarding roles in your relationship:

- Do I believe in gender-specific tasks in the home? What does my husband think?

- Do I think couples should share tasks, with each utilizing their strengths?

- How do we decide who does what? What is working for both of us? What isn't?

If you have identified areas that create conflict, in the interest of building an emotionally healthy and happy relationship, take some time to discuss one more question:

- What changes are needed so we feel we're partners, carrying an equal load as much as possible?

In addition to the issues covered so far in this chapter, one more, unfortunately, has to be addressed. Kept under wraps for many years, abuse and neglect in childhood is now well-known. Although rooted in the past, this experience can affect your marriage and needs to be acknowledged.

When Your Past Is Painful

For many people, looking back at their family life brings painful memories. Perhaps you identify. In order to function, you may have tried not to think about the influences that shaped you and produced deep emotional needs. But suppressing thoughts about your past only keeps you emotionally stuck. This in turn fuels unhealthy responses that directly affect your life and relationships.

God knows that many homes, including self-proclaimed Christian homes, produce "bruised reeds," people who are emotionally damaged by their family of origin (Isaiah 42:3). These bruised reeds in turn enter marriage, looking for someone to fill the holes in their souls. But these spiritual and emotional wounds are the kind that no partner should be expected to heal.

Describing her upbringing, Cathy talked openly about the acute loneliness she experienced as a child and its effect on her as a wife.

"My mother was a widow for many years. In order to provide for me, she worked long hours every day. As an only child, I spent most of my time by myself. When I married Richard, I thought I'd finally have someone to talk to and be with.

"So long as I went along with what he wanted, everything was okay between us. But when we disagreed over something, Richard would leave the room and refuse to talk. I immediately felt panicky and sick. The old feelings of being abandoned would resurface, so I'd go and beg him to speak to me. Many times, he wouldn't talk to me until he felt I was sorry enough."

Until we understand Richard's background, we can't know what made him withdraw and ignore Cathy. Was he uncomfortable with conflict? Did he use his awareness of her emotional hunger for control? We don't know. What we do know—and what Cathy now knows— is that her background created a deep need that wasn't met in her marriage.

A painful life produces hurts and longings, causing you to continue seeking from your spouse what you didn't get in childhood. Unless you recognize this cycle and seek healing, your emotional needs contain the potential for even more pain. This is especially true if your partner is not empathetic or willing to accompany you on your journey toward wholeness.

In contrast to Cathy's experience, Melody's husband faithfully stood by her as she journeyed through her painful past. Although her parents claimed to be Christians and never missed a church service, their explosive anger terrified both her and her twin brother, Sean. From their preschool years through high school, they were chased and beaten with belts. As small children, Melody and Sean crawled under beds and hid in cupboards in futile attempts to find a safe place. Their fear of angering their parents continued into adulthood.

Author and counselor Dr. Susan Forward asks if there is a better word than *toxic* "to describe parents who inflict ongoing trauma, abuse, and denigration on their children, and in most cases continue to do so even after their children are grown."[4]

I can't think of one.

Acknowledging that she married early to escape from home, Melody said, "I didn't realize how much anger I had because of my childhood. My husband, John, had no idea why I was so controlling, insisting that everyone do what I wanted. But he knew better than to interfere. In order to keep the peace, he rarely expressed his feelings and pretty much left me to run things in whatever way made me happy."

Dr. Forward comments, "Healthy families encourage individuality, personal responsibility, and independence. They encourage the development of their children's sense of adequacy and self-respect. Unhealthy families discourage individual expression. Everyone must conform to the thoughts and actions of the toxic parents."[5]

Expanding on her unrecognized rage that lurked like a hidden bomb primed to explode, Melody continued, "I eventually slid into a deep depression and attempted suicide several times. It was only after being hospitalized and getting into intensive counseling that I began to see the impact my upbringing had on me."

Often, the result of an unhealthy home life is a deep feeling of being unloved and worthless. These feelings don't stay dormant. Instead, they dominate how we view life and handle our relationships.

As you look back at your family of origin, could some of your personal and marital struggles be linked to a painful past? If so, let me encourage you to seek help from God and experienced Christian counselors. You can break unhealthy family ties. You can identify and replace lies about yourself with God's truth about who you are. With His help, it is never too late to heal and create a different future.

What Is My Part in Building Our Marriage?

This chapter's key verse says: "By wisdom a house is built, and through understanding it is established" (Proverbs 24:3).

God wants to give us practical wisdom that makes a difference in how we handle our problems. But to gain this wisdom, we need to take four steps that produce change: pray, look, learn, and act.

Step One: Pray

If you want your relationship to change, pray for wisdom, insight, understanding, and discernment. Christians don't have to stumble around in the dark in order to find the right answers. Ask the Holy Spirit to direct your thoughts and to bring wise and encouraging people across your path.

Wistfully hoping wisdom will descend like a cloud enveloping and changing you without any effort is just that, a wistful hope. Wisdom requires you to be proactive by looking at the truth of how you react and being willing to listen to what God wants you to know.

At times God comforted me as I poured out my frustration or hurt in prayer. Other times He encouraged me. But He has also convicted me on several occasions about my attitude and behaviors that blocked His blessing. However God speaks to you, be willing to receive what He has to say. This is a necessary growth-step on the journey toward a better marriage.

Not only do we need to pray for wisdom and understanding, we also need to ask, "God, how do You want me to apply what You're laying on my heart?" Listening and hearing without acting on what God shows us will not produce any change. In James 1:22, the apostle challenges our tendency to ignore what we don't want to see or hear. He says, "Do not merely listen to the word, and so deceive yourselves. Do what it says."

In addition, watch for those aha moments when talking with your spouse. Look for what the Holy Spirit brings to mind as you prayerfully think through a situation, when you're reading Scripture, or as you step back and observe how you interact with each other.

Keep your mental and spiritual antennas tuned in to what God wants you to learn. Then respond. Your relationship will improve, no matter how big the gap in your backgrounds.

Step Two: Look at Your Focus

I used to spend a lot of time stewing in anger and self-pity. Believe me when I tell you that it didn't get me anywhere. My circumstances did not change. My negative focus did not yield anything that reflected the Lord's presence in my life. Over time, however, it did produce two things: a desperate desire for God to do something, and a willingness to hear what He had to say, even if it wasn't easy to take.

In Psalm 51 (MSG), David cried out from his own self-induced misery, "What you're after is truth from the inside out." That remains an essential principle for growing in the Lord. Only when I was ready to listen and take responsibility for my behavior did the Holy Spirit begin to show me what I hadn't been willing to see. My negative focus powerfully affected my mood, leaving me struggling to find hope in life. My mouth spewed words of anger and discontent. And my marriage became a source of frustration rather than fulfillment.

I longed for a happier relationship, but it never occurred to me that I had a part to play in bringing it about.

Step Three: Learn to Question Negative Self-Talk

Long before psychology books were written, the Bible zeroed in on the power of our minds to affect our lives. The apostle Paul urged, "Be transformed by the renewing of your mind" (Romans 12:2). Why does he say this? Because every attitude or behavioral change begins in our mind and requires our cooperation. To re-groove our thinking and view people and situations differently, we have to start noticing and changing our automatic negative thoughts (ANTS). These thoughts pop into our minds without any effort on our part, and can be so quick and so familiar that we rarely question what they are saying.

God is not the author of any inner messages that put you down, destroy hope, or produce thoughts of doing harm to another person or yourself. These come from the pit. Knowing how we are made and our vulnerability to believing lies, Scripture urges, "Be made new in the attitude of your minds" (Ephesians 4:23). God stands ready to help us do that.

One life-transforming skill is to examine what you tell yourself. When you are discouraged or gripped by negative thoughts about yourself or your marriage, don't passively listen and believe what you are telling yourself. Instead, challenge your self-talk.

Here are some questions I use that can also help you defeat those debilitating, automatic negative thoughts.

- Is what I'm telling myself true according to God's Word?
- Is God telling me this? Is this His voice?
- Do these thoughts encourage me, comfort me, and spur me on to trust God?
- Am I listening to the lies of the evil one, messages from my past, or my insecurities?

Ask yourself these questions every time you get emotionally defeated, and you will form a new, powerful, and life-giving habit.

Step Four: Act on What God Teaches You

After God showed me the damage ANTS were doing in my life, I realized I needed to get hold of my thoughts and intentionally choose a more positive attitude. Wanting to make our marriage as happy as possible, I asked God to show me what I could do. It didn't take long before many practical steps flooded my mind. And the more steps I took, the happier I became and the happier Jim became.

If you identify with where I've been, acting on the following steps can help you change your focus.

List all of your husband's good qualities, especially those that come from his upbringing. While my husband might not agree with me on many things, I have to admit he is reliable, faithful, hardworking, and committed to the Lord—all qualities he absorbed from his family. What a difference from the list of negative qualities I chewed on when caught up in self-pity.

Focus on what you like about your husband and find ways to tell him. Re-groove your mind with happy memories, fun times, and warm feelings, and then begin to sprinkle those thoughts and feelings into your conversation.

Find ways to show love. How did you express your love in the early days? Think about what you used to enjoy doing together—riding bikes, going to ball games, renting romantic movies. If you're in a rut, break out and suggest doing some fun activities from the past.

Create new sources of mutual enjoyment. Does he enjoy gardening? Offer to help weed. Do you both like to read? Suggest a few hours browsing at a local bookstore together.

Discover what he enjoyed growing up. Did his mom make a certain pie or dish he hasn't eaten in years? Find the recipe and surprise him. Did he enjoy a particular family activity? Suggest you do it together and ask him to tell you more about his family life.

Apply Wisdom: Put Your Marriage Before Your Family

How you relate to each other's family is another area that requires wisdom in order to build a strong home. Have you ever thought about what your families expect of you and your husband? Or considered how their expectations affect your relationship, positively or negatively?

Wisdom Begins with Scripture

The primary teaching of Scripture regarding marriage is Genesis 2:24, "That is why a man leaves his father and mother and is united to his wife, and they become one flesh." One flesh is far more than the physical union of a man and woman. God intends marriage to form a new unit, a bond between two people, and a sense of identity that is separate from our family of origin. Therefore, when someone steps between couples, they are trespassing on holy ground.

Jesus added the words, "Therefore what God has joined together, let no one separate" (Matthew 19:6). Interference in marriage can come from many sources—perhaps a parent, sibling, child, or friend. In order to prevent this, we need to establish a God-ordained boundary that protects the sacred bond between a husband and wife and keeps others out.

For an emotionally healthy marriage, it is essential that no third party be allowed to come between you. Nor should a husband or wife take sides with a third party against their spouse.

Wisdom Requires Evaluating Your Family's Expectations

Some families expect their kids and spouses to join them every summer for a vacation, be with them every Thanksgiving and Christmas, and call at least once a week.

Carol, a mother of three teenagers, obeys her mother's command to call every day. Anything less brings accusations of neglect.

Judy's parents raised their children with the spoken and unspoken message: You will put us first, even if you're married and have your own family. You will come for dinner every Sunday night and anytime there is a family celebration. Judy and her husband, Sam, feel they have no choice but to show up. So do her siblings, even though they all resent their parents' expectations.

Melody, whose story was mentioned earlier in this chapter, couldn't escape her mother's dominance even in the psychiatric unit. Shortly after she entered the hospital, her mother called from another state shouting, "What are you doing in there? You are not depressed! I am coming to get you and take you home."

"Home" for Melody's mother was fifteen hundred miles away. She didn't see her daughter as an adult woman whose husband and children had the responsibility and right to take care of her. Instead, she tried once again to take control, demanding that Melody bow to her wishes.

Wisdom Requires Establishing Boundaries and Taking Action

Instead of feeling helpless in the face of family pressures, reflect on the following with your husband:

- What expectations do your parents, siblings, or children have of you?

- Be honest. How do their expectations affect your relationship?
- Does their behavior strengthen your marriage or contribute to tension between you? How?

Discuss your concerns and together agree on healthy and necessary boundaries and how you will put them into effect. If you feel you're the one who needs to set rules with your family, talk about how to say what is needed in a firm but friendly way. Remember, your goal is a healthy one: to reclaim your lives as a couple and unique family unit.

It's okay to be emotionally close to your family, but your parents must not interfere with your marital relationship. And it's not always easy keeping them out. Instead of a love triangle where you're torn between your spouse and parents or other family members, establish this ground rule: Family does not get priority. Your spouse does!

Focus on the Future, Not the Past

How you and your husband were raised affected both of you, positively and negatively. But as adults who have a relationship with the living God and who are indwelt with His powerful Spirit, you don't need to let past disagreements over family influence undermine the present.

Whether you and your spouse have been banging heads or building bonds over these issues for a few years or many decades, God is always ready to do something new in your marriage. Will you ask Him to show you what this is?

May I Pray for You?

Our wonderful, gracious heavenly Father, fill my sister's heart with a fresh awareness of the spiritual blessings You have showered upon her. Encourage her with the knowledge that she was chosen and adopted by You, and that You are at work in all her circumstances. She is Your child, and You are her perfect Father. Lord, heal any wounds inflicted by her human family or her husband's family. Let her bask in Your unconditional love. May she rest and rejoice in being Your child and let her be confident that You will provide all she needs to accomplish Your will. Amen.

(ADAPTED FROM EPHESIANS 1:3-6)

Five

His Brain Isn't Wired Like Mine

So God created mankind in his own image,
in the image of God he created them;
male and female he created them.

GENESIS 1:27

I t's perfectly logical," my husband insisted as I rolled my eyes during his explanation of how to do my tax return. "If you would file everything each time you pay a bill, you wouldn't have this annual meltdown. You'd be able to find what you need instantly. Is that so hard for you?"

For some reason, Jim's mini-lecture struck me as funny and I burst out laughing. "I'm sorry," I said. "I know it's perfectly logical for you, and I do try, but I just don't function that way!"

Understand Me, Please

When we marry, we expect to be understood. But if we marry our polar opposite, instead of living happily ever after, we often find ourselves at odds with each other. Confused and frustrated, our different viewpoints easily trigger blowups that are all out of proportion to the initial irritation.

When these conflicts happen, you might quickly find yourself muttering, "What is his problem? Why does he look at the situation that way? Doesn't he realize how his response makes me feel?" At the same time, your spouse might also be muttering, "Why is her reaction so extreme? What makes her read criticism into what I just said? Why can't she just take my statement at face value and not look for hidden meanings?"

Nature/Nurture Differences

Not long ago, there was a general assumption that differences between men and women were related more to nurture than nature. Social scientists believed and taught that girls gravitated to dolls because these were the toys provided by their mothers. In addition, girls saw their mothers have babies and care for them. This powerful modeling influenced girls to delight in babies and desire to become mothers themselves.

If circumstances were changed, went the theory, then girls would be just like boys in their interests and priorities. And, of course, the opposite was considered true. Give a boy a doll and other opportunities to get in touch with his feminine side, and he would be more outwardly emotional and caring.

Although there is much to be said for encouraging girls to excel in boy-dominated activities like sports and science and for boys to develop a nurturing spirit, the nature/nurture theory is being proven wrong.

Surprise! Our Brains Are Different

Today, using devices such as magnetic resonance imaging (MRI), positron-emission tomography (PET), autopsies, and other methods, brain research validates what Scripture asserts: God created us male and female. We are not the same. Physical and chemical differences do exist between the male and female brain, and these differences affect how we think, how we feel, and how we behave. They also account for those screams of frustration, slammed doors, and silent treatments that erupt when your calm, understanding self can no longer cope.

Right-Brain/Left-Brain Wiring

In addition to male/female individualities, other factors reveal why you and your spouse might be wired differently. Although somewhat controversial, recent studies indicate that one side of the brain can be dominant, resulting in a left-brain or right-brain processing style, although no one is exclusively one or the other.

The two hemispheres of the brain perform differently, but the dominant side is not determined by gender. You could be a left-brain processor married to a left-brain processor. If so, you're undoubtedly experiencing a more harmonious marriage than if your left-brain is married to a right-brain. We'll identify and explore these differences later in this chapter.

Personality Types

A third source of internal differences that express themselves outwardly is rooted in our personality type. An introvert often marries an extrovert and both want to change the other. A sanguine, easygoing person can frustrate a "charge-ahead-get-things-done" choleric. A melancholic sees the glass half-empty and depresses their more naturally cheerful spouse, who is viewed as unrealistic and unwilling to face facts. And if you're a leave-me-alone-to-enjoy-my-quiet-life phlegmatic, you might have a spouse who bugs you to be more outgoing.

These three factors—chemical makeup, brain dominance, and personality type—affect not only how we view life, they also affect how we view each other and how we live out our love for God and our spouse. As part of our overall goal to understand ourselves and that baffling man we married, let's look in more detail at these three areas.

His Brain Is NOT Like Mine

As a scientifically challenged female, it is not my intention to try and explain the mysteries of the brain and human development. My interest is in how these physical differences affect our relationships. However, having some idea of the innate differences between men and women is necessary if we want to understand one another.

The physical differences between both genders are self-evident. But with the cutting-edge research being done today, we now know with certainty what once was previously questioned: parts of our brains and the hormones and chemicals that flood our bodies are not identical. We have been wired to react in certain ways from the womb.

Perhaps there's some truth after all in exclaiming, "That's just like a man!" (And in men sighing, "She's a typical woman!")

After a recent marriage seminar, I watched my husband and his friend John talking animatedly. Curious to know what they were discussing, I walked over to join them.

Were they comparing notes on improving their marriages? Brainstorming ways to spend time with their spouse? No. They were talking about the merits of various airplanes. Which one could fly the farthest? How many passengers could another take? How were the cabins laid out? What seats should tall men like them choose—bulkhead or exit row?

Laughing, I said, "I can't believe that after all we've heard tonight, you two are standing here discussing planes. If you were women, you'd never be talking about such a boring topic!"

Both men grinned.

"Do you want us to be talking about our *feelings*?" John teased.

"We're men," Jim said. "Planes are much more interesting."

Whose Brain Is Bigger and Better?

Research shows that a man's brain is, on average, about 10 percent bigger than a woman's. But relax. Having a bigger brain doesn't make men the smarter sex. Intelligence tests show generally equal results between men and women.[1]

The brain is composed of various parts that perform different functions. If you're not scientifically inclined, bear with me as I describe (in simple lay terms) just one part of the brain—the limbic system.

The limbic system contains four major sections: hypothalamus, hippocampus and amygdala, cingulated gyrus, and cerebral cortex. The hypothalamus contains the brain's sex center and is sensitive to testosterone. Because females usually have 20 percent less testosterone, males generally have a stronger sex drive than women. The hippocampus and amygdala receive, process, and store our emotional memories. The cingulated gyrus oversees the process of chemical and neural connections. And the cerebral cortex is responsible for our senses, reasoning, thinking, motivation, and other functions that are all part of being human.[2]

The hippocampus and amygdala of a woman's brain enable her to more powerfully connect words, emotions, and memories than men.[3] Our capability in these areas is greater than a man's because our verbal and emotional center is larger and more active. This makes us more inclined to reach out, nurture, and talk about feelings, something most of us knew before anyone tried to look inside our brains!

Research has also discovered that a woman's brain has a greater ability to listen, comprehend, and interpret emotional needs. These physical differences are part of the reason women are famous for their intuition or sixth sense. They can process what is happening around them and can't figure out why men are blind to what is so obvious to them.

"Something is going on between Chloe and Jack," Annie said to her husband, Tony, after leaving a New Year's Eve party. "I'm sure they are seeing each other."

"No, they're not," Tony said. "You're imagining things. They were just talking and laughing together like everyone else. Besides, Jack may be separated from his wife, but he's trying to work things out with her. He wouldn't be dating someone."

A short time later it became clear that Jack and Chloe were, in fact, seeing each other. Eventually, Jack divorced his wife and married Chloe.

Describing a woman's sixth sense, authors Allan and Barbara Pease state: "It is obvious to a woman when another woman is upset or feeling hurt, while a man would generally have to physically witness tears, a temper tantrum, or be slapped around the face before he'd even have a clue anything was going on."[4]

Rather than argue about who is reading a situation correctly, simply smile, sit back, and watch. Time will tell who is right, and often it will be you.

If experiences weren't enough to prove we carry around brains that process differently, add various hormones and chemicals to the mix and our distinctions become even more pronounced. "More than seventy different chemicals have a major impact on the brain, affecting our emotions and responses," says Walt Larimore, M.D.[5] Let's look at the one that most influences a man. Then we'll focus on the one that most affects women.

Blame It on Testosterone

At six weeks gestation, boy babies are exposed to male hormones (called *androgens*) and specifically to testosterone, the man's major hormone. This makes him generally more aggressive, competitive, and assertive than women. According to Dr. Larimore, "Researchers at Georgia State University found that 'high performers' tested in each field (business leaders, politicians, sportsmen, and the like) had higher levels of testosterone."[6]

Other studies show that the more testosterone a man has, the stronger his desire for independence, freedom, and adventure. "Testosterone motivates the male to strive for separateness in ways a woman is not...It makes you want sex, but it also makes you want to be alone," says Theresa Crenshaw, M.D.[7]

Ever been baffled by why your husband is perfectly happy spending time by himself? Or why he gets excited watching grown men chase a ball and knock each other to the ground? Now you know. And if you've ever wondered why he is generally ready for sex at all hours, you have your answer. He is a man. It's his testosterone. God made him that way.

Estrogen Rules!

Have you ever been moody, felt like you were going to burst into tears, or got snappy when someone crossed you? Chalk it up to estrogen and other female hormones that flood our bodies.

As the vast majority of women (and men) know, hormones affect us in various ways at different times of the month. During the twenty-eight-day cycle, our hormones can cause some of us to feel as if we're on a roller coaster. Up one day, plummeting the next. We can even be up and down in twenty-four hours, puzzling ourselves and the man in our life.

Estrogen produces extra sensitivity to stimuli in the first three weeks of our menstrual cycle. This is our high point, when we're more likely to feel positive, enthusiastic, and sexually interested. We want to get together with our friends. We feel warm fuzzies toward little children, and we're generally more hopeful about life.

But in the last week of our cycle, our hormone levels drop. Depending on their sensitivity to this change, some women can descend into the unwelcome world of premenstrual stress or tension (PMS or PMT as it is known in certain parts of the world)—a gloomy mix of crying jags, irritability, and discouragement. It is this phase of a woman's cycle that men love to joke about:

Why did they send so many women with PMS to the Gulf War?

They fought like animals and retained water for four days.[8]

Why Doesn't He Process Like Me?

"What do you think about going to California on vacation this year?" I asked Jim as we drove to the store.

Silence.

"Can we go in July? That would be a good month to take a break."

Silence.

Irritated by Jim's lack of response, I snapped out more questions at staccato speed, culminating in a final angry demand: "Why are you ignoring me? Why won't you answer my questions?"

Frowning, Jim turned to me in confusion. In an injured voice he said, "I'm not ignoring you. I'm still thinking about your first question."

Have you had similar exchanges?

What's Your Response Rate? Fast or Slow?

Speaking generally, if you're a right-brain (RB) person, as I am, when you ask a question, you expect a fast reply. RBs process thoughts quickly, tend to be impulsive, and easily jump from one idea to another, often leaving our more methodical-thinking partner wondering what happened. We also look at the whole picture before we stop and consider the details.

Left-brain (LB) processors take time to analyze and think logically about what's before them. LBs look at the pieces first, and then put everything together to form the whole. When they do eventually speak, they have thought carefully about their response, unlike those of us who think as we speak (or in some cases, not until *after* we have said our piece).

Without realizing it, my simple question about taking a vacation in July proved a far more complex exercise for Jim than I imagined. Being a LB, his mind immediately clicked into action, drawing up a logical checklist of issues that needed consideration: *What is my work schedule like in July? Could someone cover me for two weeks? Should we drive? Will the car hold up on a thousand-mile trip? Can we afford to fly?*

Meanwhile, as the RB one in our relationship, I am growing more irritated by the minute. *What is so difficult about giving a straight yes or no answer? Details can be worked out later. Just make a decision and tell me!*

If you are a RB processor married to someone who is predominately LB, you probably have your share of similar stories. Remember, although it is tempting to say, "Oh, isn't that just like a man," not all of them fit the stereotypical LB, logical, black-and-white, problem-solving male. Nor do all women fit the stereotype of being RB, empathetic, creative chatterboxes. Perhaps you are one of those who don't fit the mold?

Which Am I? Right-Brain or Left-Brain?

Depending on the issue and your temperament, you might chalk up your spousal spats to various dissimilarities, shrug your shoulders, and simply accept that you don't see things the same way. You move on and don't let the conflicts sour your day. On the other hand, you might react with anger, hurling whatever verbal grenades come to mind. Or, if you're easily hurt, your response might be to shut down and try desperately to hide the hot tears slipping down your cheeks.

Your husband's response might make you mad
or sad, but that doesn't make him bad.

Because our styles of relating can create stress and drive us to thoughts of giving up, the sooner we grasp that we're married to someone who is unlike us, the better. Your husband's response might make you mad or sad, but that doesn't make him bad.

To discover more about how you react and interact with your spouse, try this quiz. Circle option A or B from each of the following paired statements, add them up, and see whether you're more inclined to process from your right or left brain.

A. I am more inclined to be rational and logical.
B. I tend to be more emotional.

A. I look at the details first, then the big picture.
B. I see the big picture first, then the details.

A. I am always on time.
B. I am often racing out the door at the last minute.

A. I usually think before I speak.
B. I often think and speak at the same time.

A. I think about facts.
B. I daydream and think about possibilities.

A. I am disciplined and like structure.
B. Routine bores me; I prefer freedom and variety.

A. I don't like talking about feelings.
B. Sharing feelings is essential to a satisfying relationship.

A. I do not give up easily.
B. I get discouraged and find it hard to persevere.

A. I speak plainly, saying what I mean.
B. I am expressive and enjoy embellishing a story.

A. I keep careful track of money.
B. I am comfortable having a general idea of our finances.

Totals: *As* _____ *Bs* _____

Scoring key: *As* signify left-brain processing:
       9–10 = strongly LB
       6–8 = leaning toward LB

       Bs signify right-brain processing:
       9–10 = strongly RB
       6–8 = leaning toward RB

Did you recognize how you usually think and express yourself? How would you rate your spouse? Take a moment and jot down what you've learned from this quiz about why you struggle with certain areas in your relationship. Then take time to talk to God about them, asking for further insights that will help you understand your husband *and* yourself.

Be encouraged whatever your score, even if you are off-the-charts, poles apart, and unbelievably different. The point of this brief introduction to right-brain/left-brain research is to help you recognize that if you married your opposite, your husband isn't trying to drive you crazy. He is just expressing who he is. And with God's help, you both can learn ways not only to cope, but even to shake your heads and laugh at how you come at situations from such opposite viewpoints.

Who Am I? Who Is He?

Do you ever ask yourself, "Who am I really?" Or, "Who is he?" Sometimes, accurately identifying our personality type can be difficult. But it doesn't take great powers of observation to recognize if you and your spouse are not alike. Couples who are wired differently, whose personalities don't click, inevitably clash more often than those who view life through the same lens.

Personality differences are often overlooked in the romantic dizziness of dating. But they are present all along, unnoticed, overlooked, or deemed unimportant. Once married, however, what was once tolerated can become intolerable.

> Personality differences are often overlooked
> in the romantic dizziness of dating.

A simple but accurate description of personality is "the characteristics of a person that lead to consistent patterns of feeling, thinking, and behaving."[9] These characteristics are generally established by adolescence. Slight changes might happen over time, but the fantasy of changing your spouse into a replica of yourself is not likely to happen. You can both improve your interpersonal skills, but neither of you is going to significantly change the other.

The realization that people have different personalities isn't anything new. Over twenty-five hundred years ago, the Greek philosopher Hippocrates categorized people into four groups: sanguine, choleric, phlegmatic, and melancholy. Today, many more tools exist to help people analyze their personalities.

To help you understand the role personality can play in a marriage, work through the following quiz. These questions highlight some of the general traits of the four personality types mentioned above. I think you'll discover that everyone is a mix of dominant and less-dominant traits. Knowing how your mix differs from your husband's will help you better understand him. But please understand that this is not intended to provide a thorough psychological assessment!

Using the following scale of 1–4, check the answer that best describes you:

1. Never

2. Once in a while

3. Most of the time

4. All of the time

At the end of each set of questions, total your score. Then compare those totals for all four personality types. Which type gives you the highest numbers? Where are you and your husband similar? Where are you dissimilar? Ask your husband if he would also like to take this test. If not, use a different pen color and note what you think best describes him.

Are You a Sanguine?

You love to have fun, be around people, talk and laugh. 1—2—3—4
You're enthusiastic, genuine, and share feelings easily. 1—2—3—4
You're easily moved by your emotions. 1—2—3—4
You enjoy attention; you're cheerful and caring. 1—2—3—4
You have high energy, volunteer, and encourage others. 1—2—3—4
You're creative, colorful, and spontaneous. 1—2—3—4
You like to express yourself freely. 1—2—3—4
You don't enjoy spending time alone. 1—2—3—4

Total: _____

Are You a Choleric?

You love new challenges. 1—2—3—4
You're a visionary and make things happen. 1—2—3—4
You're active and decisive. 1—2—3—4
You're independent, self-sufficient, and confident. 1—2—3—4
You're a natural leader, motivator, and goal oriented. 1—2—3—4
You like structure and organization. 1—2—3—4
You get frustrated with the status quo. 1—2—3—4
You can dominate others and push your ideas. 1—2—3—4

Total: _____

Are You a Melancholy?

You love quiet; too much noise and activity wear you out. 1—2—3—4
You're a detail person, wanting things done properly. 1—2—3—4
You're a planner and an organizer. 1—2—3—4
You don't enjoy being under pressure. 1—2—3—4
You are faithful and reliable. 1—2—3—4
You like to be on time and have a routine. 1—2—3—4
You can be hard to please and unenthusiastic. 1—2—3—4
You feel things deeply and are highly sensitive. 1—2—3—4

Total: _____

Are You a Phlegmatic?

You prefer to take life easy and not plan too far ahead.	1—2—3—4
You avoid conflict.	1—2—3—4
You don't get upset quickly.	1—2—3—4
You prefer to wait until asked to get involved.	1—2—3—4
You're competent, reliable, and objective.	1—2—3—4
You're easy to get along with, patient, and pleasant.	1—2—3—4
You don't easily identify and express your feelings.	1—2—3—4
You like to wait and see how things work out.	1—2—3—4

Total: _____

Totals: Sanguine ____ Choleric ____ Melancholy ____ Phlegmatic____

Scoring key:
Not me: 8–13
Occasionally like me: 14–19
Definitely like me: 20–25
This is *me*: 26–32

There is no perfect match of personalities that will ensure a happy marriage. In the end, your relationship is determined by how you treat each other, talk to each other, and respect each other's different personality styles.[10]

Margie, a keep-things-organized accountant, has learned this secret. She keeps a master calendar and plans annual vacations two years in advance. With a temperament mix of melancholy and choleric, she takes charge of every detail, ensuring a memorable holiday for herself and her husband, Richard. She pays the fees, makes sure they have tickets, passports, and necessary visas, and generally helps Richard stay on track.

Richard, on the other hand, is happy for Margie to take care of the details. As a sanguine, his favorite activity is meeting new people, chatting to waitresses and store owners, and participating in every available activity.

"Richard and I are wired so differently," Margie said as we discussed how so many couples marry their opposite personality type. "We don't have compatible temperaments. But after years of trying to change each other, we've found ways to get along. I just smile when Richard talks to strangers, and I don't feel I have to say much. He's an extrovert and being around people makes him happy. So why create conflict by being critical and nagging him to be more of an introvert like me?"

What Is My Part in Building Our Marriage?

Respect God's Design

The Bible tells husbands to be considerate and respectful as they live with their wives (1 Peter 3:7). This is good advice for wives also. When our husbands don't behave as we assume any normal person would, God is calling us to understand and respect that He didn't design men to be like us. Men react as men with the brains, hormones, and personalities He gave them.

Over the years, Jim and I have clashed on many issues. I couldn't understand why we saw things so differently or how we could come to totally opposite conclusions. My impulse for a long time was to think he was being deliberately difficult or stubborn. It never occurred to me that our inherent male/female wiring might be contributing to our struggles.

On various occasions when I got together with girlfriends for lunch, the conversation often turned to our husbands. Moaning that we couldn't fathom why they responded the way they did, not one of us thought to mention the obvious: We married a man, not a woman in disguise.

I've found it easy to groan, "Why can't he be more like me?" when I've felt misunderstood or my need for encouragement wasn't noticed. You may have also done your share of groaning under your breath. But think about this for a moment. What we're saying is that in order to be content, we want a man who is more like us. More like a woman.

We want a man who talks more, can describe his feelings, oozes empathy, and prefers snuggling to sports. And when he isn't like this—when he is independent and self-sufficient or keeps his thoughts to himself—we can get very unhappy and think we need to trade him in for a new model. Or at the very least, attempt to remodel him ourselves.

If you're thinking, *You're right, I have been wanting him to be more like me and expecting him to act just like my girlfriends*, then stop for a minute and realize what you're doing. Jot down your response to this question: When my husband doesn't respond as I want, how would it help me if I remembered that God created him male, not female, and that God approves of His handiwork? _____

_____

As a woman, here's a step you can take to educate your husband. Ask yourself, what can I say (gently) to help my spouse understand that God created me female, not male, and that God also highly approved of His handiwork in creating woman? _____

_____

Men and women were not designed to be identical. When God created Adam and then Eve, He created them for each other. Both have strengths and weaknesses. Both need the other. And both are valued and loved by God.

Honor Your Unique Qualities

Knowing that God created both sexes with their gender-unique qualities, we honor God when we let our husbands live out how they were designed. If they don't express their emotions easily, we can choose our response. We can resist the temptation to criticize them, demanding that they behave like us. If they are not naturally empathetic, trying instead to fix our problem, we can choose our response. We can resist flinging back a caustic comment and instead, acknowledge their desire to help. If their black-and-white decision-making leaves us frustrated, we can choose our response. We can resist scorning their perspective and instead, try to learn from it.

Does that mean we can't pray for changes in how we respond to each other? Or discuss how to talk more sensitively so we don't create deeper rifts? Of course not. But we are called, as followers of Christ, to do this in a way that shows respect for our husbands.

Instead of trying to make your husband respond to situations as you would, work with who he is. Accept his different ways of handling issues. And if for some reason you find it hard to look up to him, then choose to honor him by keeping his failures private.

I cringed while listening to Halle trash her husband over lunch with friends. Harsh and loud, she declared, "He's useless. He won't lift a finger to discipline the kids. He won't even talk to me about how they are behaving, and he leaves me to deal with them."

I felt for her husband and wondered how he must feel about her. In her frustration, Halle had ignored a foundational principle for a healthy marriage: Show respect for your husband. She shamed him publicly and became "like decay in his bones" (Proverbs 12:4).

Sadly, I have done this. You might have too. But with God's help, be encouraged that you can become like the other woman described in that same verse. You can become a virtuous and worthy wife, a crowning joy to your husband. And a delight to the Lord.

Apply God's Principles

The challenge all couples face when they find themselves clashing repeatedly is to resist the temptation to criticize, label, and blame the other. This is where we need God's help. Learning to understand your husband (and yourself) is a major stepping-stone to improving your marriage. Once you delve beneath surface differences and uncover how each of you is created, positive changes can begin.

If you're discontent because your husband isn't more like you, here are some ways to grow in understanding:

- Remember you come from different perspectives. Not only is he not your clone nor was he raised in your home, but also God designed you to have different strengths and viewpoints, different responses and priorities, different needs and experiences.

- Reflect on the truth that being male and female is God's idea and He called it good! He didn't make us this way to frustrate us but to fulfill our human need for intimacy and love. His desire is to work in us for our benefit and to change both of us so we can experience the good things He intended.

- Search out more information about the God-created physical differences between men and women. Ask God for insight into the role these differences play in your relationship and how you can adapt rather than react to them.

- Review your clashes. Try to recognize where some of your struggles come from. Are they linked to your expectations that your husband should respond as you would in a particular situation?

Celebrate What God Created

Your husband is a work in progress. So are you.

Your husband is a work in progress. So are you.

The next time you find yourself shaking your head in disbelief or gnashing your teeth in frustration at your husband's reaction, stop and think about what you've learned. And when he responds in ways that make absolutely no sense to you, repeat these biblical truths to yourself: "He is a man. God made him this way. And God declared His creation *good*!"

May I Pray for You?

Heavenly Father, You created us male and female and gave us unique strengths. Our differences were designed to bring You glory, not to create strife in our home. Knowing this, help my sister relinquish any spirit of contempt toward her husband. Give her grace to forgive hurts that have pierced her heart. Help her receive from Your Spirit a new willingness to love and appreciate her spouse. May she see him as a man who matters to You, a man in whom You are at work. May she also know the high value You place on her, a woman, created to bring both her husband and her Maker delight. Amen.

(ADAPTED FROM GENESIS 1:27; ISAIAH 43:7; COLOSSIANS 1:16)

We Don't Have the Same Emotional Needs

Each one of you also must love his wife as he loves himself,
and the wife must respect her husband.

EPHESIANS 5:33

I want to be with you," I said to Jim. Standing in the church lobby drinking coffee after the worship service, I debated whether to attend the missions meeting about to start downstairs. "We've been apart for three weeks. You've only been home one day. Even though I want to hear the mission team's report, I'd rather be with you."

"But it's okay with me if you go to the meeting," Jim insisted. "I'll see you when you get home."

I didn't go, and Jim couldn't figure out why.

When I married, I assumed happiness meant sharing mutual interests and being together whenever possible. I soon discovered that this was another romantic expectation that didn't fit my marriage.

Some couples, of course, place great value on togetherness. These lovebirds shop hand in hand, often wear the same colors, and like spending their weekends sharing chores, running errands, and generally just being around each other.

Other couples enjoy some activities together but are just as comfortable giving their spouse freedom to follow their individual interests. Because many men (and some women) crave a degree of independence even when happily married, they have no problem being on their own. Nor do they need constant emotional or verbal connection. I married a man like this.

Unfortunately, some women find themselves in a relationship that resembles an empty shell. The externals exist, but there is little inner connection of mind and heart. In this type of marriage, the wife longs for greater intimacy.

As I've talked with wives in various countries about their marriages, I've noticed a common theme: women generally want more time, conversation, attention, and affection from their husbands. Here are some snippets of what they shared:

- "I want my husband to be my best friend, but he isn't interested in talking when he gets home from work."

- "I thought marriage would be emotionally satisfying, but I feel more understood by my girlfriends than by my husband."

- "I long to do things with my husband, but he'd rather spend time with his guy friends. I feel so lonely and unwanted."

In their loneliness and desire for connection, these women fill their heart-needs through family, friends, and other pursuits.

But is this what God intends, living with constant disappointment while always conscious of what is missing? Isn't there a solution to draw a couple closer, even if they are complete opposites?

Yes, I believe there is.

Heart Differences

In his bestseller, *Wild at Heart,* John Eldredge writes, "God doesn't make generic people; he makes something very distinct—a man or a woman. In other words, there is a masculine heart and a feminine heart, and each in their own way reflect or portray to the world God's heart."[1]

According to Eldredge, a man was made to conquer (no, not like a caveman dragging a woman by her hair to his lair). Rather, a man was created with an inner drive to explore oceans, climb mountains, and soar into space. He is stimulated by risk and challenge—perhaps to start a new business or follow a deep-seated dream. He craves freedom to pursue adventure and be part of manly pursuits.

What Do We Expect?

It didn't occur to me for many years that there are profound differences between the hearts of men and women. Or that we have unique core needs. Or that our hearts thrive under different kinds of opportunities and experiences.

Beyond caring for Jim's physical needs—making dinner, doing his laundry, creating a pleasant home environment—I never thought about what he might expect or need from me as his wife. And he didn't know what I needed and expected from him as my husband.

I took it for granted, though, that Jim would instinctively know when I wanted attention and affection. Based on that assumption, I expected him to speak sweet, soothing words when I was upset, tenderly caring for my feminine heart. When this didn't happen, I wallowed in disappointment and wished he'd magically morph into someone more sensitive, more tuned in.

Someone more like me.

Perhaps you've had similar experiences?

He's Supposed to Know My Needs

One evening I asked several women in my Bible study how many of them had married assuming all their needs would be met.

Everyone laughed and chorused, "I did."

Before we walked down the aisle, not one of us in the group had understood a frequently overlooked reality: No man can possibly know or meet all our emotional needs. Why? Because he doesn't think like a woman! Nevertheless, this is the impossibly high bar we often measure our spouse against.

A common assumption among women is that our husbands should know how we feel without us having to say anything. Another assumption is that our spouse, simply by virtue of being married to us, should be able to decode our subtle messages.

When we make a simple statement such as, "Mom and I talked

today," our husbands hear, "Mom and I talked today." What we expect them to hear is, "Mom and I talked today and she isn't doing so well and I'm afraid I'm going to lose her soon and I can't handle that and can you just hold me right now because I'm going to lose it?"

Existing on another wavelength, most men find it hard to pick up what isn't clearly stated.

This common scenario between baffled, well-meaning husband and sometimes bawling wife is described humorously by a friend. In times of emotional need, she instructs her husband, "Read my mind—not my lips!"

Please Listen to Me!

When our spouse's words or actions reveal that he hasn't a clue about our current needs, hurt feelings can trigger anger, resentment, and a sudden urge to hurl whatever is handy. (Well, maybe only some of us are tempted to act like this.)

One sultry evening when we were living in Singapore, I attempted to talk to Jim about our daughter's wedding plans. It was a few months away and would take place in Oregon. Jim lay on the sofa under the ceiling fan reading the paper while I peppered him with questions.

"What should we do about hosting your family for the wedding? Where will we stay if we can't stay at our house? Can't you call and get our housing situation sorted out?"

My voice rose with each question as I glared at the newspaper, unable to see Jim's face hidden behind it. Without feedback, nods, or grunts to indicate he heard me, I became increasingly irritable. Frustration turned to fury. I grabbed the short, chubby candle off the coffee table and hurled it at Jim. Fortunately for him I was a pathetic shot. The candle fell on the floor far short of its intended target.

Horrified at my reaction, I fled down the hallway sobbing and threw myself on the bed. Jim, my phlegmatic husband, merely glanced up as I ran past and then returned to his newspaper.

With my face buried in the pillow, my inner adult lost no time in lecturing me: *Poppy Smith, what is the matter with you? You're a Bible teacher, a mentor to younger women, and look at how you behaved!*

I had to agree. I had shocked myself.

Two days later, calmed down and in my right mind, I apologized and suggested we talk about what happened. Once I explained my need to be listened to and how it felt when he ignored me, Jim apologized for being more engrossed in reading the news than in what I was saying. Rather than blaming, stewing, and assigning fault, my candle-throwing drama gave us an opportunity to grow in understanding each other. Jim learned that I needed his input. I learned that calmly stating my needs is a lot less stressful than launching the nearest object.

There Is Hope

Expecting our husbands to know our needs, and getting upset when they don't, is like expecting a blind man to read before he learns Braille. He can't do it. He is not a mind reader.

Does that mean we should forget our youthful dreams of living with our soul mate, with a man who understands us in a glance? A man who empathizes, knows our hidden desires, and instantly meets our longings?

Well, yes and no. But there is hope.

Learning to recognize and meet each other's needs is possible. But it doesn't happen without deliberate thought and action. As the authors of *The Couple Checkup* point out, "Happy marriages are not marriages without obstacles; they are marriages where couples use obstacles as opportunities to grow in their partnership."[2]

Your spouse *can* learn what you need from him, and *you* can learn what he needs from you. When this happens, and you each intentionally respond to the other, your dream of a mutually fulfilling relationship can come true. With that goal in mind, let's take the first step toward understanding those marital needs. Let's identify them.

What Are My Needs? What Are His?

Read through the following brief descriptions of common needs. At the end, add any other needs that matter to you. Then prioritize your list. You might ask your husband to do this same exercise. Or try putting yourself in his shoes and jot down how you think he might respond.

After each description, take a moment and think about how this need is met in your marriage. Is it important to you? Are you longing for more? Is there a step you could take to change this aspect of your relationship? Record your responses and use them as prayer prompters for whatever insights God brings to mind.

Affection and sexual fulfillment are frequently rated the number one need for women and men respectively. Because of this, let's give them the attention they deserve.

Affection (Women) and Sexual Intimacy (Men)

Both men and women flourish when they feel loved and accepted. For most women, affection and attention are surefire ways to ignite warm feelings toward their spouse. According to marriage counselor and author Dr. Willard Harley, affection is a woman's highest need. He describes it as the cement of a relationship, symbolizing for a woman "security, protection, comfort, and approval."[3]

Most of us feel loved when our husband spontaneously hugs and kisses us—especially if it's an expression of affection and not intended as a maneuver to get sex. The majority of men, however, feel loved and accepted when their wife is sensitive to their sexual needs.

Dr. Harley states, "Most affairs start because of a lack of affection (for the wife) and lack of sex (for the husband)."[4] He describes this as a vicious circle. The wife doesn't get enough affection so she isn't responsive to her husband's overtures. The husband doesn't get enough sex so he withholds affection. If this becomes a continuous pattern, each partner may become vulnerable to someone who is available to meet their God-created but unmet needs.

> God made men with a legitimate sexual hunger
> that we are to respect as part of His design.

Because women have less testosterone, many wives don't understand or take seriously their husband's physical need for sex. Whether it makes sense to us or not isn't the point. God made men with a legitimate sexual hunger that we are to respect as part of His design. (This topic will be dealt with more fully in a later chapter.)

God's perfect design of "women need affection—men need sex" works well when we follow it. If your husband is consistently affectionate, you probably feel loved and valued. This assurance then triggers physical and emotional changes in you, which in turn produce certain chemicals. As a result of these chemicals pouring through your body, you find yourself responding in a way that makes your perfectly normal, sexually interested husband smile in anticipation.

Whenever your husband gives you an affectionate squeeze, or you lovingly accept his need for sex, remind yourself: this is the fun part of marriage. After all, you don't really want to live like two pieces of furniture under the same roof—do you?

How would you describe your need for affection and sexual intimacy? __

_____

How well is it being met? _____

_____

What changes could you prayerfully make? _____

_____

Attention

"So how often do you think about me during the day?" Marcia asked her husband, Peter.

"When I leave in the morning, I don't think about you and the kids until I walk in the door at night," Peter responded in his usual matter-of-fact tone.

She winced at his honest comment.

"I hoped he would say something romantic about missing me and wishing we could talk during the day," Marcia told me, her eyes glistening. "Instead, Peter tells me not to call him at the office unless it's a real emergency."

Being seen as special by the man you married is important. So isn't it reasonable to assume he'd welcome your attention at unexpected moments? *After all*, you tell yourself, *I love his attention anytime and can't wait to tell him what's happened during my day.* But if you married your opposite, you have to remind yourself that your desires are not necessarily his.

As Marcia thought some more about her reaction to Peter's comment, she realized that he didn't intend to hurt her. His strong work ethic meant he focused on his job and didn't believe in chitchatting on company time.

Have you ever asked your husband how he feels about your calls during work hours? If he loves the attention and has no problem with you contacting him, enjoy these moments. But if he doesn't seem enthusiastic when you phone, don't take it personally. It might be due to his character, personality, or type of work.

When you are home and want your husband's focused attention, think about what has and hasn't worked in the past. Don't stomp off and pout when he doesn't respond as you want. Instead, take the initiative. Smile. Gently hold his face in your hands and lovingly say, "Please look at me, not the TV. I need to talk to you."

How would you describe your need for attention? _____

_____

How well is it being met? _____

_____

*What changes could you prayerfully make?*_____

_____

Admiration

Both husbands and wives need admiration. We want compliments and appreciation for serving a great dinner, caring for a sick relative, getting a promotion at work, or losing weight and looking amazing. Your spouse also wants to be admired for his skills, hard work, intelligence, or ability to provide for his family.

To strengthen your marriage, watch for what you can admire in your spouse. While affection and attention are vital for a loving relationship, words of admiration say "I notice you and value who you are." (See chapter 7 for more tips.)

Should your husband be the quiet, nondemonstrative type, share your admiration simply and sincerely. And if you're the quiet one in your twosome, don't hold back on giving your more extroverted partner the compliments he might be longing for.

If you're starving for some admiring comments, you might have to prime the pump. Be brave. Share some good news about yourself (very humbly, of course) or pirouette in front of him, asking, "What do you think? Do you like this outfit? Do I look good in it?" It might be just the prompting he needs to say what you long to hear.

If the pump still refuses to be primed, don't walk off in a huff. Continue to love him, and keep reminding yourself, *We are different: he is not my clone, he wasn't raised in my home, and he just doesn't get it!* Ask God to show you what He thinks of you instead, and thank Him for your girlfriends who do get it and have no problem pouring on the encouragement you crave.

How would you describe your need for admiration? _____

_____

How well is it being met? _____

_____

*What changes could you prayerfully make?*_____

_____

Companionship

What interests do you and your husband share? Although you might never achieve "we do everything together and even dress alike" status, learning to enjoy each other's company is an essential part of a happy marriage.

A study by the University of Chicago revealed that a lack of connection with others is physically unhealthy. Research showed that persistent feelings of loneliness raise blood pressure and increase the risk of stroke and heart attack. [5]

> When little attention is paid to each other's emotional
> needs, our human longing for companionship
> and friendship with our spouse goes unmet.

Loneliness is not confined to those who live alone. You can be married to a man who is home every night and still experience stabbing emotional loneliness. A husband can feel the same way if his wife has no time for him and no desire to share his interests. When little attention is paid to each other's emotional needs, our human longing for companionship and friendship with our spouse goes unmet.

To guard against growing apart, some counselors suggest that husbands and wives take up one another's hobbies or look for mutual interests. Unfortunately, other people's well-meaning suggestions don't always work. What if your husband is an avid golfer and you chop holes in the grass every time you hack at that obstinate little ball that refuses to budge? Or he loves fishing, but freezing in the rain while trying to attach wiggling worms to a hook turns your stomach? Perhaps a better suggestion is asking him to consider sitting quietly with you while learning to quilt. Or knit.

There are solutions that satisfy our human need for companionship, however. Here are a couple of suggestions that are simple and practical. They also work.

- Talk to each other about what you enjoy doing. Jot down as many activities as you can think of that appeal to each of you, then try to identify two or three you could do together. Once you've found a few, put them on your calendar.

- Begin to plan your dates—even if it's to sit and watch a television program you both find educational or entertaining. But spice it up in some way. Maybe change chairs? Sit very close? Make a yummy snack? Or wear something special?

How would you describe your need for companionship? _____

_____

How well is it being met? _____

_____

What changes could you prayerfully make? _____

_____

Encouragement

Scripture tells us to encourage and spur one another on (Hebrews 10:24-25). If you're married to a man whose natural bent is to encourage you when you're struggling, be thankful. But if your spouse is more inclined to see the negative in you and tells you so, watch your heart. Strengthen it daily with reminders that you are precious to God.

A negative husband may see himself as practical and realistic, offering you his views for your own good. Learn to extract what is helpful from his comments, remembering that they are colored by his personality. Train yourself to be open toward him, to listen for the meaning behind his words, and to ask God for help to control your tongue when tempted to retaliate with your own brand of helpful criticism.

Like us, men respond to support and encouragement. Instead of waiting for your husband to cheer you on or compliment your hard work, let him experience what it feels like to be encouraged. With prayer, maybe he'll learn from your example.

How would you describe your need for encouragement? _____

_____

How well is it being met? _____

_____

How could you prayerfully improve this? _____

_____

Respect

Wives are given a biblical command to respect their husbands (Ephesians 5:33). If your marriage is less than harmonious, this command can be challenging. Showing respect requires making a conscious decision not to rip into your spouse or treat him with contempt when he angers or disappoints you. It is a choice you make.

> Showing respect requires making a conscious decision not to rip into your spouse or treat him with contempt when he angers or disappoints you.

Our natural tendency is to think, *When he treats me decently, I'll show him respect. When he deserves it, I'll give it.* Treating our spouse with courtesy and respect becomes dependent, then, on how he acts. But God's Word calls us to a higher perspective, to a frame of mind possible only in the power of the Holy Spirit.

Respect is not about feelings. Nor is it conditional. It is about choosing to act in a way that says to God, "Lord, I will do what You ask out of obedience. I love You and believe You call me to do what is best."

Though it's hard to separate our emotions from what we say and do, speaking respectfully to or about our husbands is what God asks. Showing disrespect reduces your mate's worth, dismantling the very supports that keep your marriage from collapsing. Solomon said that it's a foolish woman who tears down her house with her own hands (Proverbs 14:1). He's right.

But the need for respect does not belong exclusively to husbands. It applies to wives also. Both men and women are made in the image of God. Because of our intrinsic value, each of us should give and receive respect from the other.

How would you describe your need for respect? Your husband's need? ____

_____

How well is it being met? _____

_____

What changes could you prayerfully make? _____

_____

Honesty and Openness

Can your husband read your email? Does he have your secret passwords? Do you have his? Do you each know how much the other earns or spends? Do you hide purchases, sneaking them into the house when he's not home? Does he?

Depending on your upbringing or your temperament, you might have a marriage of total honesty. You can ask your husband any question and know you'll get a straight answer. It never occurs to you to question if he's telling you the truth. You don't get suspicious about where he's been. And you never doubt that he's being honest with the family finances.

On the other hand, one or both of you might keep secrets about where you go, what you do on the computer, or how you spend your money. Perhaps you feel these areas are none of your spouse's business.

Marriage experts differ on whether a couple should have areas of privacy. For trust to be established and maintained, however, honesty and openness is essential. This demands speaking the truth rather than being evasive or deceptive. Hiding secrets, both past and present, can threaten the very survival of your marriage.

"I was strongly attracted to Tom's fun-loving nature," confessed Donna. "We fell in love quickly and had our dream wedding a year later. Shortly after we married, I discovered Tom owed thousands of dollars on his credit cards. It never occurred to me before we married to ask him about his finances. And he didn't say a word about his debts. I've always worked hard and been frugal, but now I not only feel betrayed, I might have to use my savings to bail him out."

Concerning honesty in marriage, Willard Harley says, "When honesty and cooperation exist in a marriage, you have a couple who is willing to share and to build together. They do not need to be secretive or 'private.'"[6]

How would you describe your need for honesty and openness? _____

_____

How well is it being met? _____

_____

What changes could you prayerfully make? _____

_____

Domestic Support

"My husband would just sit and wait for me to get the kids ready for church," Shelly complained. "In his home, his father never pitched in, so he acted just like his dad. After one too many Sundays, I had enough and told him I needed help even if his mother never had any!"

Both husbands and wives work, whether out of the home or inside it. Each gets tired and stressed from endless demands, and each longs for support from the other. Whether it's a word of thanks for working so hard, helping to get a meal on the table, or rounding up the kids and calming them down, a marriage thrives when both spouses express appreciation to the other.

As a wife, watch out for signs that your husband is particularly tired. Be sensitive to his concerns about the job market, his fears of getting stuck in a dead-end job, or his feelings of inadequacy as a father or spiritual man. Each of these observations is an opportunity to sensitively express your support and appreciation.

If you're a mother, speak well of him to your children. No matter what struggles the two of you might have, your children don't have to hear about it.

And when your spouse does step in and help, respond with love and affection, not a cynical, "Well, it's about time." A sour reaction will only discourage him and make him think twice about helping again.

Being ignored, taken for granted, or even criticized for some failing as a homemaker or mother creates pain. So does feeling that your husband has appointed you chief parent, head janitor, and nonstop chef. The desire to be valued is central to our makeup. If it isn't being met, ask God to help you model domestic support and seek His direction concerning how to ask your husband for it in return.

How would you describe your need for domestic support? _____

_____

How well is it being met? _____

_____

What changes could you prayerfully make? _____

_____

Spiritual Connection

Godly Christian women around the globe dream of marrying a man who will not only share their desire for God but will also lead them closer to Him. Women pray for this man, plead with God for him, and watch with mixed delight and dismay as their girlfriends walk down the aisle on the arm of a saintly male.

A single friend in her late thirties didn't hesitate to share her prayer request with a group of us. We erupted in shrieks of laughter as she declared, "I want a man who is hot, holy, honest, and heterosexual."

God has put this longing in the hearts of women who honor Him. It is normal. And it is good.

If your husband isn't a follower of Jesus, Scripture says to pray and zip your lips so "they may be won over without words by the behavior of their wives" (1 Peter 3:1). But if your husband claims to follow Jesus and isn't perfect in his attitudes, choices, and priorities all the time, your challenge is to grow in grace toward him.

Marrying a believer in Christ does not mean we marry the finished product. He is raw material in the hands of the Spirit. So are you. So am I.

> Marrying a believer in Christ does not mean
> we marry the finished product.

We will cover this topic more fully in a later chapter. In the meantime, focus on the blessings God has given you through this man who is a "work in progress."

How would you describe your need for spiritual connection? _____

_____

How well is it being met? _____

_____

What changes could you prayerfully make? _____

_____

Prioritize Your Needs

Now that you've read a brief description of these common needs, which ones stand out as most important to you? Take a few minutes to prioritize them on a scale of 1 (least important) to 10 (most important). As a last exercise, ask your husband to do the same thing. If he won't join in, do it for him based on your best guess. Show him what you think, and then ask him to comment on how you prioritized his needs.

Relationship Needs	*My Priorities*	*His Priorities*
1. Affection		
2. Sexual Intimacy		
3. Attention		
4. Admiration		
5. Companionship		
6. Encouragement		
7. Respect		
8. Honesty and Openness		
9. Domestic Support		
10. Spiritual Connection		

Other needs that matter to you:

_____

_____

What Is My Part in Building Our Marriage?

Now that you've identified what you want most out of your relationship, let's look at some ways to make this happen. If you know what matters most to your husband, praying for insights into how you both can experience deeper satisfaction with each other is the first place to begin.

No matter how daunting this might seem, be encouraged. Even though it takes two people working together to radically improve a marriage, God has given you the power to make significant changes. His help is available. And you have access to all the grace, forgiveness, and hope you'll need as you intentionally respond to your husband's needs—and share your own.

Essentials for a Satisfying Relationship

To start the process, here are three essentials for a more satisfying relationship. The first two essentials, Check Your Attitude and Practice Acceptance, focus on your response to your husband. The third essential, Take Action, provides practical steps for taking care of your own longings as a woman created by God.

1. Check Your Attitude

In discussing the difficulties of opposite personalities, author and counselor Rebecca Cutter states, "Their *attitude* toward their differences—not their differences—creates a barrier to intimacy."[7]

The apostle James homes in on our attitudes when he asks, "What causes fights and quarrels among you?" (James 4:1). What would you say? Unfortunately, in many marriages, the answer is, "My needs are not being met. What I want is not happening."

James 4:2 then points out one reason we get irritated with each other: "You desire but do not have." He is right. We don't get angry or sullen and threaten to walk out when we get what we want, but we might react this way when our desires, goals, or needs are neglected. If so, we need a Jesus attitude adjustment.

Think about how Jesus received and loved imperfect people and ask yourself, *Do I need an attitude adjustment?* Most of us do from time to time.

*Think about how Jesus received and loved imperfect
people and ask yourself, Do I need an attitude adjustment?*

If you know God's Spirit is speaking to you, don't hesitate to respond. And if you're muttering, "I'll meet his needs when he meets mine," consider Jesus' words: "Even the Son of Man did not come to be served, but to serve" (Mark 10:45). If your attitude needs changing, ask God for help. He will gladly empower you to respond differently.

2. Practice Acceptance

Most women expect acceptance and love from their husbands. Ironically, many wives find it hard to give acceptance and love in turn, especially if their spouse fails to live up to their expectations. In response to their feelings of frustration, many embark on a spousal remodeling project, but they rarely succeed. No matter how hard wives try to change their husbands, few men are willing to let them succeed.

Accepting your husband's failure to be perfectly in tune with your needs or to fully satisfy your longings isn't easy. Nevertheless, you are called to love him regardless of his lack of awareness or sensitivity.

Your mate's male mind, personality, or background might make him seem emotionally and verbally handicapped to you, but he is still a person worthy of love, a person who has legitimate needs that God asks a wife to meet.

Jesus demonstrated that true love is not a variable emotion but an act of the will. In light of this, what adjustment do you need to make to love and accept your humanly imperfect husband?

3. Take Action

- Review what you regard as needs in your marriage. Are they essential? Or are they wants or desires? If it's unlikely your husband can fulfill these, look for other legitimate sources of satisfaction. Cultivate close friendships, do things in groups, heighten your awareness of God's loving presence.

- Talk to your husband about the importance of being sensitive to each other's needs. Tell him what you want from him and how good it makes you feel when he responds and how it hurts when he doesn't.

- Ask him for a hug when you want one. Make the first move. Initiate sexual intimacy. Plan for it by being rested. Prepare as if for a special event. Esther spent a year being prepared for her big encounter (Esther 2:12). How about carving out ten minutes?

If you and your husband were to individually rate your marriage, it is likely that his level of satisfaction will be higher than yours. As women, that tells us something. We are made to bond on a level that meets the longings of our hearts.

Some marriages experience this. If yours doesn't, allow the Lord to meet these longings. By regularly coming into His presence and pouring out your heart to Him, your soul thirst for acceptance and understanding will be abundantly filled by the only One who is able to love you, not only perfectly but forever.

In addition, seek the affirming company of family and dear friends who know all about you and still love you. Your intimate heart-needs do not have to go unmet. The God who created you will also provide for you in every way.

May I Pray for You?

Lord, teach Your precious daughter how to find her deepest satisfaction in You. Your love is better than anything life can bring. Help her trust in You as she follows Your example through serving and accepting her husband. As she delights herself in You, give her grace to believe that You will meet her needs and empower her to live for You. May she look for Your goodness to be poured out on her as Your faithful, never-ending love continues to surround her. Amen.

(ADAPTED FROM PSALM 63:3; PROVERBS 3:5; PSALM 31:19)

Seven

When I Say This, He Hears That

The tongue has the power of life and death.

PROVERBS 18:21

We drove the first mile in silence, enjoying the sunshine and scenery. Then I decided I needed some conversation.

"Jim, let's talk about something," I suggested.

"What do you want to talk about?" he asked.

"I'd like to chat about anything. What's on your mind?"

"Nothing."

I stifled an exasperated sigh. "Surely you're thinking about something. Let's discuss that."

"Well, I'm not thinking about anything so I have nothing to say. But if you want to talk, go ahead. I'm happy to sit quietly and enjoy the view."

Jim continued driving, a contented smile on his face. Frustrated and annoyed, I stared at the windshield wondering why communication was so complicated. After all, I wasn't asking for an in-depth analysis of his thoughts. I just wanted to talk!

What Is Good Communication?

Most of us would describe good communication as talking and listening. But there's another key component. In *The Couple Checkup*, the authors define communication as "the dynamic process through which people try to convey meaning to one another."[1]

In every exchange, it isn't enough to just hear words. The person listening has to understand what the speaker means, which isn't as simple as it sounds, even if the conversation is between husband and wife. Tone of voice, choice of words, and your previous history together are clues that help you grasp each other's meaning.

After baking some scones that came out of the oven hard, flat, and pale brown, I asked Jim if he'd like one. Glancing at them he asked, "Are they stones?"

His question struck me as funny, as well as an accurate description of my culinary offerings. Laughing at his comment, I agreed that they did look like stones. To my surprise, Jim said, "I didn't call them stones. I said scones. You misheard me."

Fortunately, what could have led to hurt feelings ended in both of us learning another important principle: Make sure you check what you thought the other person said.

Hear What Is Meant

Good communication is when you both accurately understand what you mean through your choice of words. More than grasping meaning, however, good communication is like a bungee cord that pulls you together. The benefits are both internal and external. Your God-imbedded longings to be known, understood, and supported are met. As you keep sharing thoughts, dreams, and fears, your early love and trust becomes an even stronger tie, binding you together as you face life's inevitable struggles and storms.

Of course, this is assuming you are able to talk at a deeper level than whether you prefer chow mein or fried rice at your local Chinese restaurant. Opening your heart and being vulnerable requires a level of trust where you both feel safe from personal attack. If this isn't the case in your marriage, don't despair. Regardless of past hurts, you can work toward letting yourself be known. This is what God wants, and He will help you learn and apply the necessary skills.

In my longing to be changed by God, I've prayed many times, *Lord, please show me why Jim and I find it so hard to understand each other. When I say one thing, he hears another—and vice versa. We need Your help.*

As I've pondered this common difficulty between couples, I've discovered several contributing factors, ranging from the understandable male/female differences to selfish and sinful attitudes and habits.

Miscommunication is a relational
minefield in many marriages.

Miscommunication is a relational minefield in many marriages. To avoid unnecessary explosions, you need to learn what might be contributing to the problems between you. In addition, finding ways to defuse misunderstandings can help lower your stress level and increase your ability to cope. A benefit I have personally appreciated.

Why Is Communicating So Difficult?

Your Spouse Is Not You

Most of us marry expecting our spouse to mirror our style of conversation. When they don't, it's easy to feel hurt or dismissed. If we're overwhelmed by any of these emotions, it doesn't take long to react. Frustration easily leads to fiery quarrels.

But men also find themselves baffled by how women communicate and what we expect from them. Frustration is not the sole domain of women.

Unless we replace our negative interactions with more positive responses, persistent feelings of anger or hopelessness ultimately lead many husbands and wives to give up trying to relate. This may be followed by either shutting down verbally or becoming habitually sarcastic, by looking elsewhere for emotional connection or mulling over the pros and cons of divorce.

Perhaps you have experienced this unfortunate spiral.

Men and Women at Work

Studies on male/female interaction in the workplace report that women typically seek a sense of connection with their coworkers. They want rapport and are more likely to build it by showing family photos or sharing vacation details. Women strive for consensus rather than dominance when making decisions. And they generally find it easier to ask for help or directions.

In contrast, men tend not to ask for assistance, preferring to figure things out for themselves. They like problem solving and using logic to conquer challenges. When giving reports, men typically stick to the facts, avoid unnecessary details, and cut to the bottom line. They are also able to make hard decisions without being swayed by their emotions.[2]

These differences in communication styles don't stay in the workplace. They go home with us.

Women-Talk

Have you ever seen your husband roll his eyes as you regale him with all that happened in your day? Or have you found yourself giving irrelevant details (in his estimation) and going off on rabbit trails only to realize you've forgotten your point? This is the way many of us talk.

When we catch up with friends over coffee, we know we'll have a rapt audience for our tale. We want to hear every detail of their stories as well. Mere facts are not enough. We crave colorful, expressive storytelling. But talking to our husbands in like manner can drive the average male to huddle behind his newspaper or compulsively click the remote.

However, you might think you're married to a savvy spouse who knows all about women-talk. With eyes locked on yours, he listens without interruption to every rambling word, nods appropriately, and can even recall what you said should you doubt he's listening. But don't be fooled. All the while he's likely crying out, *How much longer is she going to keep talking?*

Men-Talk

While women explain, expand, and lengthen, men shorten.

"Yes." "No." "Fine." This to-the-point style may leave conversation-starved wives feeling shut out. Sometimes, desperate for more information, women beg, insist, and demand, only to be met with blank stares. "What do you want me to say?" their husbands ask, genuinely confused. "I've told you everything."

Another situation that creates sparks is when you and your husband are driving along and you both know you're lost. If you have ever pleaded with a man to stop and ask for directions, you'll appreciate this question. "Why did Moses spend forty years in the desert?" The answer? "He refused to ask for directions."[3]

For a deeper look into the mysteries of the male mind, check out the following advice from men:

- Don't ask us what we're thinking about unless you're prepared to discuss such topics as sex, sports, finances, or cars.

- Come to us with a problem only if you want help solving it. That's what we do. Sympathy is what your girlfriends are for.

- If something we said can be interpreted two ways and one of the ways makes you sad or angry, we meant the other one.

- You can either ask us to do something or tell us how you want it done. Not both. If you already know best how to do it, just do it yourself.

- Ask for what you want. Let us be clear on this one: Subtle hints do not work. Strong hints do not work. Obvious hints do not work. Just say it![4]

Here's another piece of hard-won advice from one male to another: "No man is truly married until he understands every word his wife is *not* saying."[5]

Personality Talk

If you and your husband have different personalities, expect to have different communication styles. Learning about these differences, respecting them, and trying to understand why you handle things the way you do is how to make a marriage work.

You might be an extrovert who loves to comment on whatever pops into your head, while your spouse is naturally quiet or speaks in a way that shuts you out. Learning to communicate can be tough, but this is not an insurmountable problem. If you can learn another language, develop interior-decorating skills, or master a computer program, you can learn and put into practice new ways of talking that draw you closer.

Consider intentionally looking for ways to help your husband learn to expand his cut-and-dried vocabulary. You might try approaching him at a warm moment and tell him the kind of words you want to hear. Explain your need for more than one-word responses and how you would feel if he could expand his sentences and talk a little more.

In their fun and informative book, *Getting Along with Almost Anybody*, authors and speakers Florence and Marita Littauer illustrate a creative way to deal with this familiar problem. One morning, Marita served her husband, Chuck, a gourmet breakfast—fresh-ground coffee, made-from-scratch buttermilk pancakes, bacon, and just-squeezed orange juice. When she asked him how it was, he responded, "Fine." To Chuck, with his quieter temperament, this was adequate praise. But Marita needed a more enthusiastic response to feel her efforts were appreciated.

Snatching up his half-eaten plate of food, Marita walked to the kitchen, waited for a moment, and then returned. She set the plate in front of Chuck and asked again, "Chuck, how's the breakfast?"

With a big smile he responded, "This is the best breakfast I've ever had in my entire life!"

Commenting on how our personalities affect our communication style, Marita declared, "Chuck was communicating to me out of his personality, and I was hearing him from mine."[6]

Different Doesn't Have to Mean Difficult

Evaluating how you talk and how you expect your husband to respond is an important first step toward defusing misunderstandings. Look at this brief summary of each personality type and see which style most closely resembles yours.

> *Sanguine*: Talkative, expresses feelings, gives many details, interrupts, speaks rapidly, thinks while talking.

> *Choleric*: Impatient with chitchat, speaks with purpose, gives facts, is logical and decisive, uses verbal skills to persuade.

Melancholy: Cautious, analytical, sees imperfections and says so, suggests ways to fix rather than flex with a situation.

Phlegmatic: Speaks calmly, thinks before speaking, talks when he/she has something worth saying, listens without interrupting, has a quiet sense of humor.

Do you recognize yourself? Which style is more like your husband? If your communication brings frustration, recognize your different traits. Instead of demanding he be like you, look inward and ask yourself a few questions:

- Am I expecting a level of interaction that comes naturally to me but not to him?

- Am I waiting for warm, effusive words to flow from his lips when he's an analytical perfectionist who always sees room for improvement?

- Am I pushing him to be more decisive like me…to stop procrastinating?

- Am I resenting his in-charge manner, wanting him to relax and go with the flow?

Take time to think about how your personalities affect your relationship. Pray for the willingness to work with how your husband communicates rather than condemning him, but be sure to ask God to show you how to do this in His power. Share what you're learning with your husband and expect these insights to have a positive effect, drawing you closer.

How Do I Communicate?

Good communication takes work. It also requires an awareness of what you say and do that creates problems between you.

Look through the following conversation killers and see if you're guilty of some of them. I know I am. Check off the poor habits you're brave enough to acknowledge. Then go back over the list marking those you see in your husband.

Conversation Killers

1. *Interrupting.* Jumping in before the other has finished speaking because your mind is racing with added details you must share. Or you disagree and want to set things straight.

> Me: ❏ Frequently ❏ Occasionally ❏ Never
> My husband: ❏ Frequently ❏ Occasionally ❏ Never

2. *Changing the Topic.* This can be intentional to avoid an issue. Or it can signify impatience and taking control of the conversation. It can also cause confusion when your spouse thought you were talking about one topic and you are suddenly discussing another.

> Me: ❏ Frequently ❏ Occasionally ❏ Never
> My husband: ❏ Frequently ❏ Occasionally ❏ Never

3. *Kitchen-Sinking.* A psychological term for bringing in every issue that upsets you when the conversation started out with one. Frequently includes references to mothers, other relatives, friends, and long-buried disagreements.

> Me: ❏ Frequently ❏ Occasionally ❏ Never
> My husband: ❏ Frequently ❏ Occasionally ❏ Never

4. *Tit-for-Tat Complaints.* One complaint triggers a return attack. Can be an automatic defensive tactic, signaling an unwillingness to consider if your partner has a point.

> Me: ❏ Frequently ❏ Occasionally ❏ Never
> My husband: ❏ Frequently ❏ Occasionally ❏ Never

5. *Mind-Reading.* Making assumptions about what your partner is thinking. Reading into what he's saying and his motivations for saying it.

> Me: ❏ Frequently ❏ Occasionally ❏ Never
> My husband: ❏ Frequently ❏ Occasionally ❏ Never

6. *Being Right.* Correcting your partner as they describe an event. An inability to let an inaccurate but inconsequential comment pass without jumping in. Causes embarrassment and irritation when done in public.

> Me: ❑ Frequently ❑ Occasionally ❑ Never
>
> My husband: ❑ Frequently ❑ Occasionally ❑ Never

7. *Threats and Ultimatums.* "If you do this, I will…" Sometimes erupting out of frustration and hopelessness. Can also be a control tactic evoking fear and compliance. Destroys trust and builds resentment.

> Me: ❑ Frequently ❑ Occasionally ❑ Never
>
> My husband: ❑ Frequently ❑ Occasionally ❑ Never

8. *Always and Never.* Exaggerates the frequency of a behavior we don't like. Causes the hearer to feel attacked and their efforts unappreciated.

> Me: ❑ Frequently ❑ Occasionally ❑ Never
>
> My husband: ❑ Frequently ❑ Occasionally ❑ Never

9. *Criticizing, Judging, Nit-Picking.* Finding fault with the other's appearance, behaviors, choices. An irritable spirit that criticizes easily. The inability to lovingly accept the other.

> Me: ❑ Frequently ❑ Occasionally ❑ Never
>
> My husband: ❑ Frequently ❑ Occasionally ❑ Never

10. *Shutting Down, Withdrawing, Refusing to Speak.* A way to avoid emotional pain when feeling attacked or overwhelmed. Can also be used to show disapproval and to punish.

> Me: ❑ Frequently ❑ Occasionally ❑ Never
>
> My husband: ❑ Frequently ❑ Occasionally ❑ Never

Can Bad Habits Be Conquered? Yes!

I'm sure you saw a few behaviors listed that you'd prefer not to acknowledge. James, the brother of Jesus, understood how we struggle with our tongues and affirmed what we know: "We all stumble in many ways. Anyone who is never at fault in what they say is perfect, able to keep their whole body in check" (James 3:2).

If you find it hard to admit some faults, let me ask you a question: Have you ever said something you wish you hadn't? I doubt anyone can claim verbal perfection. At times, all of us say things we would like to retract.

According to Scripture, Jesus never took back what He said or apologized for His words. He was perfect in every way (Hebrews 4:15). None of us are in that category. However, with Christ in us by His Spirit, we don't need to stay stuck in negative and hurtful ways of speaking that might come from our parents' modeling, our personality, or unresolved bitterness.

Even if your spouse isn't as sensitive as you'd like, it is still possible for you, as a Christian wife, to intentionally speak to him with patience, love, and gentleness. What you say, and how you say it, can change. With God's help you can learn to respond differently, practice self-control, and guard your words.

Begin with Yourself

Any change in how you communicate with your husband must begin with you. Even though you cannot change how he speaks to you, you can ask him to be more respectful because you are his wife. However he chooses to respond, you aren't responsible before God to make your spouse alter his language or tone of voice.

Instead of focusing on your husband's faults, which generates only anger or despair, God asks two things of you: Allow Him to soften your heart toward your husband so you are not poisoned by bitterness, and faithfully pray for your husband's heart to soften toward the Lord and toward you.

As we begin looking in more detail at how to change the way you communicate with your husband, let me encourage you to take a moment to pray for humility and honesty with yourself and with God. Next, write down what you think are *your* three most frequent communication faults—those unhelpful responses that you want to be rid of. Refer to the list above as needed.

_____

_____

If you're aware of some ways your husband hurts you when talking together, name them below. You can stew over these and allow them to fuel resentment. Or you can let them stir you up to pray for God to change your husband's heart and hurtful habits.

_____

_____

By intentionally praying for these changes, you'll be reminded to watch for signs of answered prayer. But be patient. God's answers often take time and will require persistent change on your part. As you keep cooperating with His Spirit, however, your changed responses will become a powerful witness that speaks loudly—even if you never say a word.

Check Your Heart

Good communication is more than deciphering what your husband means. It is hindered or helped by the condition of your heart. How you feel toward him colors what you think he is saying.

In the earlier years of my marriage, I wasn't even aware of how I automatically assumed a hurtful meaning when my husband said something. Reacting in anger, I retaliated with cutting words, never stopping to ask if I understood him correctly. I looked for evil, not good.

Is this where you find yourself at times? Proverbs 11:27 says, "Whoever seeks good finds favor, but evil comes to one who searches for it." The truth of this blunt statement can't be dismissed. You can find good or evil in what your husband says, or doesn't say, if you look for it. Thankfully, this sin-infected pattern of finding fault, judging, and criticizing can be overcome with God's help—if you're willing. In addition, you can learn new ways to communicate and experience the Holy Spirit's power to transform your thoughts and words.

Develop Tongue Control

The Bible tackles the need for tongue control head-on. With clear principles for how we should speak to others, and especially to our spouse, we cannot claim ignorance as an excuse for yelling and blaming or using our tongue to inflict pain.

Unfortunately, too often within marriage we drop the standards of politeness that rule our other relationships, permitting ourselves to say things we'd never dream of saying to a dear friend. We might blame our spouse, our gender, our temperament, or our personality for our nasty behavior, but let's be honest with ourselves. At such times, we are choosing not to control our tongues. If we claim that Christ is Lord of our lives, we must measure what we say against the plumb line of Scripture.

Declaring that we do have a degree of control over our tongues, the apostle Paul writes in Ephesians 4:29, "Do not let any unwholesome talk come out of your mouths." The book of Proverbs also addresses the strategic role our tongues play in building others up or tearing them down:

> The words of the reckless pierce like swords,
> > but the tongue of the wise brings healing.
> > > (Proverbs 12:18)

> A gentle answer turns away wrath,
> > but a harsh word stirs up anger.
> > > (Proverbs 15:1)

> The lips of the righteous nourish many,
> > but fools die for lack of sense.
> > > (Proverbs 10:21)

> Those who guard their lips preserve their lives,
> > but those who speak rashly will come to ruin.
> > > (Proverbs 13:3)

From the mouth of the righteous comes the fruit of wisdom,
but a perverse tongue will be silenced.
(Proverbs 10:31)

If the words that come out of your mouth create problems in your marriage, let me encourage you to focus on these five proverbs. Ask God for ears to hear and eyes to see what you need to change. Don't shrink back or fight against Him. Jot down what you sense God is saying to you.

_____

_____

What is your response? _____

_____

_____

Spend a few minutes writing down the verses that stood out to you. Put them on sticky notes and attach them to your bathroom mirror, your dashboard, your wallet, your fridge. Take the words into your heart, repeat them over and over, and keep at it until you see the change you long for. Live out the words of Psalm 119:10-11:

I seek you with all my heart;
do not let me stray from your commands.
I have hidden your word in my heart
that I might not sin against you.

What Is My Part in Building Our Marriage?

Deep in thought, Paula stopped scrubbing the baking potatoes she was fixing for dinner and stared out the kitchen window. "Dave," she said softly to her husband, "what do you think about me applying for a promotion? It would mean more money, but I'd have to work longer days. Do you think you could help with making dinner more often? And taking Miriam to her ballet practice and Steve to baseball? And... Dave, are you listening to me?"

Turning around she saw Dave, eyes glued to the screen, listening intently to a sports reporter giving breaking news about his favorite team. He hadn't heard a word she'd said.

Recognize What Not to Do

It doesn't take much imagination to see what could happen next. Paula, hurt at being ignored, might yell at Dave for not listening or caring about her. Or she might retreat further inside her head, irked that her latest effort to talk went nowhere.

A third possibility is that Paula could stop, reflect on what went wrong, and learn from it.

For better communication, keep in mind this simple checklist:

- Make sure you have eye contact. Yelling down the hallway or up the stairs sets the stage for irritable responses.

- Speak at a level your husband can hear comfortably. If you drop your voice, whisper, or look away, it's hard to hear, especially with noise in the background.

- When you want something, make your request clearly and directly.

- Wait for an answer to your first question before asking another.

- Make sure you have your husband's attention before you start speaking.

Learn What Works

Every marriage needs frequent positive exchanges if it is to thrive. Giving words of support, appreciation, and admiration regularly creates a closeness and warmth that nourishes your relationship. So does laughing together, learning to listen, discovering how to ask for what you want, and developing other conversation-changing skills.

If you've struggled in your marriage, wondering if you will ever be able to talk to your husband without going crazy, here are some skills you can learn and put into practice. To help you increase the number of positive exchanges between the two of you, adopt these new ways of conversing. After a time, you'll begin to notice the results. You'll find yourself filled with a sense of wonder and gratitude that you really can hear and understand each other.

Commit to Listening

"Jim, why don't we invite people from church over for lunch on Sunday? It's been a while since we did that. What do you think?" I asked.

"No, I don't want people over," Jim responded.

"What do you mean? You're an elder and the Bible says elders are supposed to be hospitable. How can you say you don't want to ever have people over again?"

Jim sighed. "I didn't say I don't *ever* want to invite people over again. It's just that I have a demanding day on Monday and would prefer to relax this weekend and get prepared."

After asking the question, I assumed I knew what Jim was thinking, jumped to a wrong conclusion, didn't ask clarifying questions, and wrapped it all up with an unkind dose of criticism. And as a woman who reads God's Word, I even quoted Scripture for good measure.

Speaking to our husbands like this isn't how we build closeness and trust. In fact, it might well drive them deeper into their verbal cave. If you want to entice your spouse to talk, commit yourself to these principles of listening:

- Wait until he is finished speaking before you jump in.

- Before answering, check your assumptions about what he meant.

- Ask clarifying questions: "Could you explain what you meant by…? Did I understand you to say…?"

- Train yourself to pray as you listen, asking God for the ability to hear what is being expressed through your husband's words, emotions, and body language.

Greater detail on the role good listening skills play in resolving conflicts can be found in the next chapter.

Cultivate Positive Words

Affirming your husband, telling him how much you appreciate who he is and what he does, or praising and encouraging him might come naturally to you. But in a marriage tinged with disappointment, even the most demonstrative woman can hold back. If you want your relationship to improve, this is a mistake. Giving positive strokes pays great dividends.

"Positive messages are the soul food that nourishes a marriage," writes author and counselor Sandra Gray Bender in *Recreating Marriage with the Same Old Spouse.* "They help couples get through difficult times. They create joy in the good times."[7]

Various reasons can be cited for an absence of warm and supportive exchanges in a marriage. Perhaps you're not particularly verbal, or you feel self-conscious at the thought of praising your husband. Perhaps you fear he will react negatively. Maybe it has been so long since you encouraged and affirmed each other you've decided it's easier to stick with less-personal comments.

Whatever your reason for withholding encouragement, if you want to build a closer relationship with your husband, start cultivating this practice. Remember, we all need words of affirmation, appreciation, and encouragement. Spoken sincerely, these words help soften any hard feelings between you and build rapport.

Understandably, you hope to receive similar messages in response, but again, be patient. Remember your purpose is to honor God and do what lies in your power to build your marriage. With that in mind, here are some suggestions from Dr. Bender to help you speak life-giving words.

AFFIRMATION: WHAT DOES YOUR HUSBAND DO WELL?

Does he hold a steady job? Fix what breaks? Pay bills on time? If you can't think of anything, ask God to open your eyes and your heart. Then verbalize what you see. Affirmations acknowledge the effort your spouse put into something and show that you recognize his good qualities.

Start your affirmation focusing on his action, followed by your feeling. Here are two examples:

- *You did* a great job (landscaping/building/cleaning) and I feel (proud/relieved/supported).

- *You are* (hardworking/a man of integrity/compassionate) and I feel (cared for/loved/ overjoyed).

APPRECIATION: WHAT DOES YOUR HUSBAND DO THAT PLEASES YOU?

Appreciation tells him that you enjoy something he has done—maybe going out of his way to buy your favorite tea or picking up a magazine he knows you like. A simple "thank you" shows you aren't taking what he does for granted, but consider saying more.

"Thank you for caring enough to stop and buy me my favorite tea. It was very thoughtful of you. I especially appreciate you doing this today when you're so busy."

"I really appreciate you stopping to pick up that magazine, especially as it has that recipe I told you about. You are so good at remembering details."

By adding information about what you specifically appreciated, not only will he feel loved, but he'll also know how to please you again.

PRAISE: WHAT DO YOU ADMIRE ABOUT YOUR HUSBAND?

Does he have a good sense of humor? Is he a careful money manager? A great dad? Praise is making a positive evaluation about him and verbalizing it. If you notice how good your husband looks in his new shirt, or how patient he is when coaching your son, or how he generously gives time to a neighbor in need, give him a smile, a hug, and words of praise.

Even if he protests or seems uncomfortable, don't hold back from making this a regular part of your interaction. Underneath, everyone enjoys sincere compliments.

ENCOURAGEMENT: WHERE DOES YOUR HUSBAND NEED YOUR SUPPORT?

Is he feeling like a failure as a husband or provider? Does he need assurance that you love him? Is he waiting for you to cheer him on, being his support at a difficult time? As a woman who longs to honor the Lord, what words can you say to lift up your husband today?

Proverbs tells us, "The tongue has the power of life and death" (18:21). How are you using this powerful instrument that God has given you? To bless and speak words of life into your husband's heart? To whisper expressions of love, putting your arms around his waist and assuring him of your trust?

Or are there some changes you need to make? Some habits that you need to break?

Scripture urges Christians to be encouragers, to inspire with courage, hope, and confidence. This is a privilege afforded every godly wife. You can be God's voice, a reminder to your husband that the Lord will never leave him alone in life's difficulties.

Even if your past communication patterns have caused much heartache, they can change. With God all things are possible. Believe this, and then watch Him work.

May I Pray for You?

Heavenly Father, You tell us to set a guard over our mouths, to give gentle answers that defuse angry feelings, and to not let any unwholesome words cross our lips. I pray for my sister who struggles with saying harsh and hurtful words. I ask that You give her a heart that longs to be at peace with You and with her husband. Give her a hunger to speak only words that build up her husband, words that assure him of her love in spite of past struggles. Confirm to her heart that this inner change is possible because Your power is always available. Fill her with hope and delight in Your grace and goodness. Amen.

(ADAPTED FROM EPHESIANS 4:29; PROVERBS 15:1; PSALM 141:3)

Eight

He Handles Conflict One Way, I Handle It Another

Get rid of all bitterness, rage and anger,
brawling and slander, along with every form of malice.
Be kind and compassionate to one another,
forgiving each other,
just as in Christ God forgave you.

EPHESIANS 4:31-32

Pessimistic about our chances of finding somewhere to stay late on a Friday afternoon in Florence, Italy, Jim decided we should stop for the night miles outside the city. Pointing to a less-than-appealing motel nearby, he said, "Let's stay there."

My heart sank as I stared at the dingy building. I hadn't come all the way from America to stay in something that looked like a third-rate motel in a seedy town. "Jim, that isn't what I had in mind," I wailed. "I want something quaint, charming, European, not *that.*"

Jim turned the car around without a word and headed to Florence.

Our dream vacation in Europe, beginning on Germany's Romantic Road, fizzled into annoyance as we got locked in the bumper-to-bumper traffic circling the city. And I was the cause.

"Forget seeing Florence," Jim muttered after thirty minutes. "I've had enough. We are getting off this freeway at the next exit and going wherever it takes us."

Fortunately, the road we randomly took led to a charming Italian village where we found a room at a quaint hotel overlooking the central piazza.

"Don't you think this is much better than that ugly motel?" I asked Jim sweetly.

He didn't say anything. But he did smile.

Conflict Happens

If you assumed that you and your spouse would never disagree and argue over who gets their way, or believed that happily married Christian couples never have conflicts, you've probably been sadly disillusioned. Conflict happens. It is normal, understandable, and occurs in every marriage, both happy and unhappy.

> Conflict happens. It is normal, understandable, and occurs in every marriage, both happy and unhappy.

How you and your spouse feel about conflict and react to it, however, determines whether your disagreements will become opportunities to grow together or obstacles that drive you apart.

"I DIDN'T KNOW THAT ABOUT YOU!"

Healthy conflict has benefits. Handled in positive ways, conflict helps you know more about your husband and yourself. You discover what's important to both of you and why. You also get to see how your respective upbringings, backgrounds, personality type, and life experiences have shaped your perspective.

"I'M USED TO HIDING MY FEELINGS."

Not all couples view conflict as an opportunity to gain helpful insights and grow closer. Many prefer to ignore their differences, hoping they will disappear.

Even though they are aware of tension between them, the thought of addressing their differences arouses fear-filled memories from past painful relationships. Prompted to protect themselves from these uncomfortable feelings, they repress rather than express their true reactions.

My friend Diane, a bubbly blonde, shared that she and her husband, Larry, had similar upbringings: neither were raised in emotionally healthy environments. They both had highly demanding, critical, and controlling mothers. Learning that the only safe way to survive was to obey and be silent shaped their automatic response to conflict.

"Larry was not allowed to complain or express anger. He had to keep it all in, be the 'good boy,' and always do what he was told," Diane said. "He's the same today. When he gets angry with me, he doesn't complain or show his feelings. His voice does get a little more intense, but that's the only clue he gives. He never even raised his voice at our sons if they did something wrong.

"My parents got mad and yelled at my sister and me. They hit us, but we weren't allowed to show anger toward them or we got hit some more. I learned to stuff my rage early on and became an expert at hiding my feelings. I've since learned that isn't healthy, so now I tell Larry how I feel if I'm really upset.

"We still slip into our old habits at times, stuffing our anger and not admitting we're upset with each other. But we're learning."

Perhaps this is your style?

"It's safer to stuff it."

In contrast to either healthily resolving your conflicts or unhealthily choosing to ignore them, you or your husband might have opted for a third route. You find yourselves with a stack of unresolved issues that fuel an ever-simmering cauldron of irritation. When the cauldron boils over, causing an explosion, you recognize once again the deep divisions between you. And you wonder how you got there and what to do about it.

It is a mistake to think you have no choice but to accept what happens. You do have choices.

If differences of opinion catapult your husband into attacking you—whether verbally or physically—it's understandable if you're nervous about what might happen if you speak up. And so you acquiesce, believing that it is more pleasing to the Lord to live in uneasy peace with your spouse than to address the problems between you.

You stay and pray and hope for change, even though you recognize that your situation is emotionally or physically unhealthy for you and your children.

Or perhaps you fight back with a vehemence that nearly equals your husband's.

We will look later in this chapter at how to discern the difference between common conflicts and abusive behavior as well as what steps you can take.

What Causes Conflicts?

There are many reasons for finding ourselves at odds with our spouse. See if you recognize some of them from this run-in with my husband.

Drooling over the cover photo of my favorite home-decorating magazine, I developed a major case of covetousness. Masses of daffodils filled flowerbeds near the front door of a charming cottage. *That's what I want,* I told myself. *I'm going to plant dozens of bulbs right by the front door. Next spring our entryway will look just like that.*

It didn't occur to me to discuss my plans with Jim who is the *real gardener* in our family.

A week later, carrying my bucket of bulbs along with the necessary tools, I headed toward my chosen spot. Visions of yellow daffodils danced in my head.

"Where are you going to plant those bulbs?" Jim asked as he pruned the blueberry bushes nearby.

"Right here," I said, setting my bucket against the house. "I saw a gorgeous photo of masses of daffodils, and I want this area to look just like it."

Jim shook his head, clearly not sharing my enthusiasm. "I don't want them planted there," he said. "They look great for a few weeks, and then they die. And you never get around to cleaning them up."

I had imagined sunny yellow flowers bobbing in the breeze, charming everyone who came to the house. But Jim saw only dried up yellow heads and stalks like dead weeds, spoiling his yard. Neglected by the one who had originally pleaded for them, their removal would inevitably become his responsibility.

Check the Basics

Jim and I got upset with each other on this occasion for several reasons. As you read what I learned from my missteps, see what applies to the conflicts you and husband get into.

I DIDN'T DISCUSS MY PLANS BEFORE TAKING ACTION.

As the gardener in our family, Jim listens to my input. But he doesn't necessarily act on it. When you both care about an issue, make sure you discuss specific plans with each other. If you've agreed on who is responsible for various tasks and one spouse has the freedom to make decisions without consulting the other, there's no problem. If not, failing to get agreement can lead to unnecessary arguments.

WE BOTH WANTED OUR OWN WAY.

My goal was to see lovely, graceful daffodils dancing by our front door. When Jim protested, I became angry. That's what happens when our goals are blocked.

Neil Anderson writes, "A wife and mother may say, 'My goal in life is to have a loving, harmonious, happy family.' Who can block that goal? Every person in her family can block her goal—not only *can*, they *will*!"[1] But no one can stop your goal to become the woman and wife God calls you to be. Except yourself, of course.

Do you have a strong will and a tendency to react quickly? If so, battles over which one of you is going to get your way can be triggered by even minor issues. Stopping to ask God if what you want is what He wants and if you're going about it in a way that honors Him can defuse conflict and allow you to respond with grace.

WE BOTH BELIEVED WE WERE RIGHT.

Initially, everyone views a situation from their own perspective. This is normal. The difficulty comes when we don't agree on what to do when those perspectives are in conflict. It comes down to three choices:

1. Continue squabbling about who is right and who should give in

2. Negotiate a compromise

3. Defer to the other's wishes

After some strong protests on both sides, Jim and I negotiated a compromise. With my fervent promises to faithfully remove every dead daffodil, Jim agreed I could plant them in another part of the front yard. Not in the exact spot I wanted, but close enough to make me smile every time I walked out the door.

WE HAD DIFFERENT FAMILY MODELS.

Our different upbringings shaped our expectations of how conflicts get resolved. Jim had never heard his mother assert herself. She did what his father wanted. I had never seen my father assert himself. He did what my mother wanted. We both assumed the other would yield. After all, that was what we had seen.

We couldn't fathom why we came at issues from opposite viewpoints. Frequently demoralized, I often wondered if Jim and I would ever be able to agree or even understand why we were so different. Once I gained the insights shared in this book, I started to understand *why* we approached issues differently.

Now I'm able to recognize where Jim's views come from (most of the time) and can say, "That's your background speaking. Your Midwest values." Even occasionally, "I hear your father talking!"

Of course, he also recognizes what influences my reactions and tells me, "That's your British upbringing; we don't do things like that here in America." Or if he's in a particularly teasing mood, "You sound just like your mother!"

What's the result of this? How does it help? By learning more about each other and discovering ways to compromise instead of clash, our relationship took a great leap forward. We are more sensitive to one another, more willing to accept that we have understandably different points of view, and more willing to let each other be who we are.

WE HAVE DIFFERENT PERSONALITIES.

Each personality type has strengths, but our weaknesses are what trip us up. If you're a spontaneous sanguine married to a strong phlegmatic, the likelihood of conflict between you is high. While your mind buzzes with fun ideas that you want to implement right away, your phlegmatic spouse sees your plans as unrealistic and wastes no time telling you. His intention isn't to hurt your feelings. He's just letting you know his opinion.

Other personality combinations also ignite sparks, making it important to know how you and your husband are wired.

Why Do You React Like That?

Our basic personality type plays a significant role in how we react to our differences. But we are not locked in to how we react because of our personality. If we live by the Spirit, we can deal with irritations in ways that show respect and strengthen a sense of togetherness. We don't have to "gratify the desires of the flesh," responding out of our flesh-driven tendencies (Galatians 5:16).

> Our basic personality type plays a significant
> role in how we react to our differences.

To help you catch the typical reactions of each personality when not operating under the Spirit's control, reflect on the following. Which responses do you identify with? Which seem to fit your husband?

Sanguine: Often hot-tempered, vocal, easily frustrated, changeable, undisciplined

Choleric: Wants to be in control, domineering, knows best, can be bossy and impatient

Phlegmatic: Procrastinates, avoids conflict, indecisive, easily pushed around

Melancholy: Wants everything perfect, hard to please, critical, moody, sulks, unforgiving[2]

Who Is Perfect?

Looking at this depressing list of human weaknesses is a reminder that not one of us is perfect and without sin. "All have sinned," Paul declares. "All fall short" (Romans 3:23). That includes you and me. It also includes our spouses.

Your husband's flesh-driven reactions might seem far worse to you than your own. But watch out for a sense of superiority. We need God's forgiveness for our less-than-loving reactions as much as our spouse does.

The fact that we have all sinned is not the end of the story, however. Through our blood-bought relationship with God, we have peace with Him. We don't have to be slaves to our personality weaknesses or our backgrounds. Nor do we need to give Satan power to keep us mired in feelings of failure. We are on a journey to maturity, secure in Christ's promise to be with us through our struggles and mess-ups, and ultimately to make us like Himself (Romans 8:28-29).

You don't have to dread condemnation or shame because you haven't been the perfect wife. Instead, determine to learn all you can about how to handle conflict in ways that honor God. By doing this, you can claim His promise that those who honor Him, He will honor (1 Samuel 2:30). You will also be amazed to find that God gives you an increasing love and appreciation for that man who is so not like you.

What Is My Part in Building Our Marriage?

Defuse Conflict

KNOW WHAT FRUSTRATES YOU.

You leave coffee cups lying around. There's one in the bathroom, one by your bed, one sitting by the kitchen sink. Your spouse groans, "Do you have to leave your messy cups all over the house?" You, in turn, can hardly stand it as you stare at the mess in his office. Piles of documents cover the carpet. Every surface lies buried under haphazard layers of files, books, magazines, old newspaper clippings, and long-lost official records.

Translate this illustration to what irritates you. And what irritates your husband. Either one of you might be messy—tools scattered around the garage, makeup bottles and tubes cluttering the bathroom counter, yard a mess, dirty dishes piled high. The other is tidier, perhaps even a perfectionist who is driven to distraction by anything out of place.

The differences that create conflict are too many to list, but here are a few common ones:

- Is one of you talkative and the other more of a hermit? Does one of you want vacations in the sun and the other hates being hot?

- Do you like to listen to one kind of music, but he prefers another?

- Does one of you start and finish projects, but the other starts and leaves them unfinished?

- Is your taste in décor clean, fresh, contemporary, while his runs to a comfy black, cast-off recliner?

Recognize any irritants so far? Take a moment and write down some of the issues that cause you to fume. _____

_____

Now write down some of your husband's pet peeves. _____

_____

The point of this exercise is not to stir you up and set you off. It's to help you keep specifics in mind as you find ways to defuse everyday differences. Being aware of how your personalities click or clash allows you to spot potential flash points. Then, instead of blundering into a fight, you can backtrack, calm things down, or turn the issue into an opportunity to learn more about why you see things so differently.

No one has to settle for a marriage of constant bickering. If you're willing to learn conflict-defusing skills and practice them on the minor annoyances that pop up in every marriage, you'll be well prepared for handling your more serious issues.

When you choose to look for solutions rather than how to win at all costs, you'll build rapport and strengthen the bond between you. You'll also feel better about yourself as you actively work toward your goal of being a wife who pleases God.

RECOGNIZE THE DIFFERENCE BETWEEN CONSTRUCTIVE AND DESTRUCTIVE ANGER.

Not all anger is wrong. Even Jesus got angry. Mark 3:1-6 says that when Jesus saw the indifference of the crowd in the synagogue to a man's suffering, He looked around at them in anger. Their stubborn, callous hearts aroused Him to righteous anger. Ignoring the crowd's disapproval of healing on the Sabbath, Jesus said to the man, "Stretch out your hand." After the man stretched it out, "his hand was completely restored."

Paul writes, "'In your anger do not sin': Do not let the sun go down while you are still angry, and do not give the devil a foothold" (Ephesians 4:26-27).

Anger that moves you to action is the right response to injustice. As a strongly felt, God-given emotion, anger can prompt us to reject evil and work for what is right. This is as true in marriage as it is in eliminating social injustices.

Anger can be a tool for good, for positive change, and for honoring God. But nursing unspoken and unresolved anger is like being hooked up to a poisonous IV drip. If allowed to seep into your soul, it can corrupt and destroy.

Anger can be a tool for good, for positive change, and for honoring God. But if allowed to seep into your soul, anger can corrode and destroy.

Unresolved anger triggers fights, feeds feelings of despair, and fosters self-justifying excuses. However vindicated you feel at stewing in anger or spewing it whenever provoked, you're called to deal with what is in your heart and not give the devil an opportunity to use your bitterness.

If you've used anger destructively, as most of us have, those past responses don't have to define how you will resolve conflict in the future. By improving your ability to grasp what your husband says and learning to express yourself so he understands your viewpoint, destructive exchanges can be eliminated.

Learn How to Talk

When either one of you exclaims, "We need to talk," you'll find the following practices helpful in moving you closer to the goal of a happier marriage. However, as with all inner and outer changes, each new behavior is a challenge that requires prayer and the willingness to look honestly at how you contribute to your disagreements.

Be prepared for many occasions where you'll desperately need more patience, perseverance, and self-control than you usually have. This is God's work and He will pour all you need into your heart by His Spirit (Philippians 2:13).

Change is never easy. Accept that when you try these approaches you'll probably trip up, have to take two steps back, and start again. Although your new responses will be evident to your husband, there's no guarantee that they will change his behavior. The important thing is that *you* will be doing what is right before the Lord. Here are some steps toward that end:

CALM YOURSELF.

As soon as a conflict erupts and you recognize you're upset, ask yourself some clarifying questions:

- What is this about?
- Is my reaction justified or am I making a mountain out of a molehill, blowing off steam because it makes me feel better?
- Was it his intention to upset me?
- Am I unfairly assuming he can read my mind and should know how I feel?
- What am I telling myself about him that inflames my self-talk?

COMMIT TO DISAGREEING WITH RESPECT.

- Agree to no blaming or name-calling.

- Define the problem you're dealing with and stick to that issue. Do not mention other times this happened and how you felt then, and now this is too much!

- Don't tell the other what to do or what they meant. That's mind reading.

- Don't tell the other what they should think, feel, or want. That's dominating.

- Show respect and a willingness to learn the other's viewpoint by careful listening.

- Summarize what you believe is the other's position without scorn, ridicule, or criticism.

CHECK WHAT YOU THINK YOU HEAR.

To avoid misinterpreting what your husband said, ask what he meant. Some couples use a card labeled *The Floor.* When one of them has the card, that person has the floor and can speak without interruption. (It's probably wise to use a time limit.) Once finished, the listener states what they heard, allowing the speaker to clarify. This exchange can be repeated until both understand the other. Then the original listener gets *The Floor.*[3]

COMMUNICATE HONESTLY.

If you feel attacked, have the courage to call a time-out. Stop the conversation. Speak up calmly and say, "I heard you say…and it made me feel…Is that what you meant?" Once again, give your husband time to respond without interrupting or defending. In this way you can keep track of each other's feelings and correctly interpret what you're saying. Be sure to also give your husband permission to stop the conversation if he wants to clarify something you said.

STAY ENGAGED.

Do you feel you're being judged? Are you hearing subtle criticism?

Instead of stewing or stomping off in a huff, stop and deal with it. Stay engaged by expressing your concerns. Ask for clarification: "I heard...Am I misreading what you meant, or is there a problem we need to discuss?"

If your husband feels *he* is being criticized and reacts negatively to something you say, stop and ask what he heard. Rather than reacting with verbal jabs or shutting down, staying engaged builds trust and creates understanding. Proverbs puts it well:

> Slowness to anger makes for deep understanding;
> a quick-tempered person stockpiles stupidity.
> (Proverbs 14:29 msg)

BE ALERT TO HIDDEN AGENDAS—YOURS AND HIS.

In addition to words and feelings, conflicts frequently have hidden agendas. Communication expert John Gottman writes, "The hidden agenda means that while it seems that one issue is being discussed, there is actually another issue at stake, one hidden or implicit."[4]

Hidden agendas are like proxy wars. You debate an issue, but the truth is, what you're arguing over is not the real problem. Your disagreement covers something deeper. Sometimes these hidden issues haven't been faced because they are too threatening.

If your quarrels leave you feeling unloved, unvalued, or unwanted, could they be linked to more significant problems than the surface issue at hand? Ask God to give you insight and the courage needed to face what is really upsetting you.

ESTABLISH CONSTRUCTIVE HABITS.

- Every time you get upset, ask yourself, *Will my anger bring about what I desire—a better relationship, less stress, a solution?*

- Change "he should" statements whenever they come to mind. Learn to say: "It would have been nice if he..." Or "I wish the situation were...But it isn't."

- Grow personally and spiritually by speaking truth to yourself: *Life does not always turn out as I wish. But with God's help, I can cope. There are solutions. I can learn new responses.*

- Work as a team. Talk about how you can settle your differences so you both win. Be creative and brainstorm possible solutions. Evaluate which ideas you each like. Take responsibility for the solution.

When Differences Become Destructive

Signs of an Abusive Relationship

Author and counselor Leslie Vernick states that an abusive relationship is where "one person continually seeks power over the other and uses abusive tactics (whether physical, verbal, sexual, or economic) to control and intimidate."

Debbie has often experienced verbal abuse.

"Frank calls me filthy names," Debbie said through her sobs. "No one would believe how he is at home because he's so quiet and pleasant at church. When I disagree with him, he loses his temper, says horrible things, and calls me an ungrateful, unsubmissive wife. I feel awful about myself."

In Monica's case, the abuse didn't stop with name-calling.

"Chuck slapped me across the face again last week," Monica whispered. "I know he didn't mean to hurt me. Maybe it was my fault. I guess I must have provoked him. What hurts just as much, though, is that when I raise the issue of going back to work, he attacks me and says I'm useless, stupid, and could never manage without him taking care of me."

Debbie and Monica represent the pain many women live with, even in so-called Christian marriages.

"Power-seeking abusers don't love their victims in a godly way," Vernick says. "The abusers' focus is only on *their* feelings, *their* wants, *their* needs, and *their* preferences. Their victims function merely as objects that can help to fulfill those desires, wishes, needs, and so on. When an abuser fails to attain these goals, rage often results."[5]

A healthy marriage permits both parties to speak up and express their thoughts and desires. You can differ with each other without fear of being verbally or physically attacked. But in an unhealthy marriage, one partner (statistically, more often the man) insists on being in control. He makes the decisions and tells you exactly what to do. He might decide what you can wear, who you can spend time with, what family members you can visit, and how the money is spent. You have no power to change what he wants.

Even if your spouse claims to be a Christian, a controlling relationship is not a healthy or Christ-honoring relationship. Husbands and wives are of equal value to God. Each is to treat the other with the respect and honor due those for whom Christ died and in whom He lives.

When the apostle Paul called wives to submit to their husbands (Ephesians 5:22), he was not giving men the right to act as dictators, demanding obedience to their every wish. Nor was he saying to Christian wives that they have no choice but to accept cruel words, control, and whatever selfish, sin-fueled behavior their husbands direct toward them.

In place of this distorted understanding of what men can demand from their wives and what wives have to accept, Paul challenges husbands to grow beyond their human tendencies. Using the highest standard he could draw on, Paul points out God's expectation of a married man: "Husbands, love your wives, just as Christ loved the church and gave himself up for her" (Ephesians 5:25). That level of love is possible only with His help.

Signs of a Christ-Honoring Relationship

As God's chosen people, both husbands and wives are to exhibit compassion, kindness, humility, gentleness, and patience. We are to bear with each other's weaknesses, forgive our grievances, and love one another (Colossians 3:12-14).

Marriage, as designed by God, is a precious relationship that requires both you and your husband to be self-sacrificing, to take tender care of the other, and to lovingly accept each other—no matter how different you are. God's desire is for you both to thrive, to become the people He designed you to be, and to fulfill all the good works He prepared in advance for you to do (Ephesians 2:10).

But what if your marriage is not a growing, healthy relationship? What if your differences result in angry fights or resentful silence? What if your fear is overwhelming, forcing you to do whatever your husband demands? Are there any steps you can take?

Practical Steps for Dealing with a Destructive Relationship

Please understand that the following information is not intended to replace professional counseling. These comments are given to raise your awareness of the differences between normal marital conflicts and destructive relationships.

Understand God Does Not Condone Abusive Behavior

If you tell yourself that God expects you to do whatever your husband says, you are believing a powerful lie. If your spouse asks you to sin, would you do it? If he asked you to believe a lie that went against God's Word, would you swallow it? When wives are told to submit to their husbands in everything as they do to the Lord (Ephesians 5:22-24), there is a standard to apply. Is the request one that honors and pleases the Lord? Would Jesus ask it of you?

Another lie from Satan is to trick you into believing you deserve the painful words or abusive actions thrown at you. An even worse lie is that God is punishing you because of something you did.

This is a satanic distortion of God's character and an attack on what Christ accomplished on the cross. Believe the glorious words of Scripture: "There is now no condemnation for those who are in Christ Jesus" (Romans 8:1). As His child, God's Spirit convicts, points out where you've sinned, and offers cleansing and restoration. In contrast, Satan condemns, discourages, and overwhelms with a sense of worthlessness.

Cling to the truths you know about God. What He asks of you is always with your good in mind because He is for you. He delights in you as His daughter and calls you precious. He knows all that is happening in your life, and He hears the cries of the oppressed.

As you dwell on these encouraging truths found throughout the Bible, ask yourself, *Would this compassionate God approve of the abusive, ugly, destructive behavior in my home? Would He endorse what my husband says and does to me?*

Take Responsibility for Change

Making changes can be scary, but allowing a damaging situation to continue doesn't help anyone. Nor does it honor God.

If you believe your conflicts fall into the abusive category, begin to pray for specific direction from the Lord. Jesus teaches that if you have something against another person, you are to go privately to that person and point out the offense (Matthew 18:15-18). This applies to all relationships, including your marriage.

You are also told to share your struggle with one or two others if your husband dismisses your words. These mature people might be a Christian counselor, pastor, or wise friends who can come alongside while you work through the changes that need to happen. Although it seems more comfortable to keep your situation a secret and get by as best you can, this isn't God's answer. Hiding the truth out of fear, false loyalty, or shame simply keeps you stuck. Facing the truth allows God to begin working on your behalf.

Should you decide to speak to your husband, think through the details carefully. What is the best time and situation? What words will clearly and calmly express your feelings? What are the specific behaviors you want to see changed? What consequences will there be if there is no change?

Before taking *any* action, I recommend you read Leslie Vernick's *The Emotionally Destructive Relationship*. Educate yourself about abuse, call a hotline, and seek the help of a professional counselor experienced in these issues.

Make Pleasing Christ Your Heart's Priority

When Christian men submit their hearts, desires, attitudes, and thoughts to the Lord and choose to live with reverence for Christ, their behavior toward their wives will never be hurtful and abusive. The same truth applies to you and to me.

Instead of brooding on your differences and allowing them to poison your attitude, turn your mind toward God. He will provide all you need to move forward. Invite Him to flood your heart with confidence that He can and will work in you and act on your behalf. Ask Him to fill your mind with truth that eradicates the lies you've believed about your situation. Pray for new ways to respond to those conflicts that inevitably arise between two very different people.

May I Pray for You?

Lord, please fill Your precious daughter with a heightened awareness that You are with her and that You know and understand her circumstances. When the tears flow, assure her that You care about her marriage and her husband. May she hear Your words of love and affirmation: "Do not fear, for I have redeemed you; I have summoned you by name; you are mine." Flood her with such a deep love for You that she is able to respond to stress and conflict with Spirit-given self-control. And may she experience what only You can provide by Your Spirit, a love that endures long and is patient and kind.

(ADAPTED FROM 1 PETER 5:7-11; ISAIAH 43:1;
GALATIANS 5:22-23; 1 CORINTHIANS 13:4-6)

Nine

I Think "Bargain,"
He Thinks "Bankruptcy"

I know what it is to be in need, and I know what it is to have plenty.
I have learned the secret of being content in any and every situation,
whether well fed or hungry, whether living in plenty or in want.

PHILIPPIANS 4:12

Money needs to be saved for a rainy day," Jim said.

"But what if it never rains?" I asked. "Then what?"

Raised by frugal, hardworking, plain-living folks in the Midwest, Jim was unprepared for a wife who didn't see money in quite the same way. Predictably, our different views catapulted us into one of the leading causes of divorce—fights over money.

Disagreements are inevitable when two people with different parental models, personalities, and spending habits tackle the touchy subject of finances. Pledging to live together for richer or poorer and to share all our worldly goods is easier to say than to practice.

A poll by American Express suggests that money produces more stress and spats in a marriage than any other issue. They found that among professional pairs under age thirty, a huge 72 percent have argued while talking finances.[1]

Longer married couples aren't immune either. You and your spouse might have agreed how to spend and save early in your marriage, but arguments can erupt later when life takes unexpected turns. Stress over being let go from a job, a scary diagnosis from your doctor, or a painful family crisis can leave you reeling over how to cope with these sudden financial demands.

After asking and answering the obvious questions (Do we have enough to pay for these sudden expenses? What about the long-term costs? Did we save enough for emergencies?), it's an easy jump to begin blaming each other for financial predicaments. "If you hadn't bought... If you would stick to a budget...If you earned more...If you..."

Perhaps you're fortunate enough to have adequate savings and can cope with unexpected rainy days. On the other hand, you might be barely making it from month to month. Whatever your financial status, money issues lie behind a lot of marital misery.

Facing Facts

Joe Larson, a certified Christian credit counselor, says, "Financial difficulties and the stress that accompanies them are the leading cause of divorce." In addition, he identifies divorce as one of the main factors behind filing for bankruptcy. Commenting on the irony of couples ending their marriage because of financial problems only to be plunged deeper into debt, Larson asks, "What benefit can a divorce have on your finances?"[2]

The harsh reality of divorce is that the lower wage earner usually suffers more financially. In the majority of cases, this is the woman who may have left the workforce, at least temporarily, to care for children.[3]

Statistically, nearly 30 percent of recently divorced or separated men experienced an improvement in the ranking of their adjusted household income. The comparable statistic for women was less than 10 percent.[4]

Other research shows that divorced women with children are four times more likely than married women to have an income that is under the poverty line. Although 10 percent of families in the U.S. are headed by a woman, 40 percent of poor families have a female head of household.[5]

Will divorce solve your financial troubles? Probably not. So what choices do you have if your marriage is coming apart over money? Marriage counselors and financial advisers give the same counsel: Sit down and communicate with each other. If you clash over cash, start talking about it. Talk about your money, his money, all your income and your outgo. Plan a budget. Set up a savings plan. Determine, for the sake of your marriage, to find solutions.

Before looking at solutions, however, you need to know what motivates your fights over money.

Why Do We Fight Over Money?

Previous Experiences

Have you ever asked yourself what money means to you? Look back at experiences in your life, either as a child, teen, college student, or young person working and providing for yourself. Can you recall any times of panic or fear associated with not having enough money? Your emotional reaction to that possibly traumatic experience might still lurk deep in your memory. Given the right stressors, you could relive anxious, uncomfortable feelings in struggles over finances.

"Joe always told me that our savings belong to both of us, but when I wanted to remodel our kitchen, he wouldn't consider it," Tracy said. "After I promised to use all the money I had in my own meager savings account, he reluctantly agreed to cover what I couldn't pay for. When he told me later that I had to pay him back for the money he put into the remodeling, I started crying. And I couldn't stop.

"Even while I was sobbing, I kept asking myself what was going on. Why was I so upset? After a while the memory of being single, completely broke, and having no family to turn to for help flooded my mind. All the emotions I felt back then swept over me, and I just kept crying until there were no more tears. I had no idea how that experience had scarred me or how it had created such high anxiety about not having enough money.

"Later, when I was able to talk to Joe, I explained where I thought my reaction came from. He assured me he would always make sure there was enough money so I needn't fear being penniless again." Tracy smiled as she wiped her teary eyes. "And the best thing was he apologized for saying I needed to pay him back."

Your previous experiences with money might not set you up for the kind of emotional meltdown Tracy experienced. Maybe your strongest reaction has been no more than acute disappointment when you realized you couldn't afford to splurge on a snazzy outfit that caught your eye. Nevertheless, money means something to each of us. It carries a deeper personal significance than being merely a way to buy what we want.

Personal Meaning

In order to find common ground in spending, saving, and setting financial goals, let's begin by looking at what money means to you both. Our goal is to uncover the root of your struggle.

Remind yourself of some basic causes for your differences: you're not clones; you weren't raised in the same home; your views of money were highly influenced by events that occurred long before you met each other.

One well-known television evangelist whose childhood was marked by poverty and humiliation vowed he would never be poor again. After much blessing on his ministry, he bilked his followers out of millions of dollars, using their donations to live a life of luxury. Money meant significance, success, personal value. His response to these inner drives eventually landed him in prison, convicted of embezzlement.[6]

The financial circumstances of our growing-up years have an inevitable impact. How our parents handled their assets contributes to our view of money and the power it has over us. By sharing your experiences and discussing your individual perspectives on money, you'll understand why you differ.

To begin, take a few minutes to reflect honestly on the following possibilities. Jot down whatever insights come to you. Note which description most closely resembles your viewpoint. Which seems to describe your husband's?

Money as the path to fun

Without plenty of spending money, would life seem grim? Does the idea of downsizing, choosing the simple life, buying only items you need rather than want, eating at home, and skipping the latest sale at your favorite store leave you feeling deprived? Are your credit cards a magic wand, opening the door to retail-therapy-induced endorphins? How would your husband answer this?

My viewpoint: _____

My husband's: _____

MONEY AS SYMBOLIZING SUCCESS

Is it important for you to drive a new car? Live in a neighborhood as nice as your peers? Buy quality clothes? Are these outward symbols of success and status important, providing a sense of significance and worth? How would you feel about yourself and the value of your life if these were to disappear? How would you feel about your husband (or yourself if you're the primary wage earner) if he could no longer afford to provide for you at this level? How would your husband answer these questions?

My viewpoint: _____

My husband's: _____

MONEY AS SECURITY

Do you get more pleasure saving than spending? Do unforeseen major expenses make you anxious? Are you often concerned you might not have enough for that "rainy day," even though you put money away regularly and tap into it only for emergencies? Does your view of money hinder or help you to give generously to God's kingdom? What is your husband's view?

My viewpoint: _____

My husband's: _____

MONEY AS POWER

Do you and your husband have an equal voice in your financial decisions? Or does the one who contributes the most money hold veto power over the other? Are finances used to control, to assert and maintain authority, so family members are dependent on the favor of the one with the money? Do you believe that the major wage earner should call the shots where financial decisions are concerned? What would your husband say?

My viewpoint: _____

My husband's: _____

Money as _____

There are many other ways to view money: as an opportunity to give to the needs of others, as a means to support God's kingdom, as recognition of your work and capabilities, as provision for your needs. How would you describe what money means to you?

My viewpoint: _____

My husband's: _____

If you felt uncomfortable acknowledging your perspective, remember, you don't have to share this information with anyone else. Also, God already knows your heart, your motives, and your thoughts. He isn't shocked. He knows we are frail creatures who wrestle with mixed motives and divided hearts—sometimes selfishly greedy, other times selflessly generous.

Unresolved Tensions

Another step toward discovering what fuels your fights over finances is to identify which issues keep cropping up. Look at the list below. Do you recognize areas you can't agree on? Check off what applies to you and add any others that come to mind.

- Setting a budget—actually sitting down and doing it
- Agreeing on the budget you set
- Living within your budget
- Not having enough money to spend
- One spouse spending more than the other
- Splurging instead of saving

- How much to save, where to invest it, who does the investing
- Who pays the bills
- How to reduce the bills
- How to agree on what to buy
- Giving a percentage of your income to God regularly

Other issues: _____

_____

Personality Differences

Did you know that your personality affects how you handle money? And that a one-size-fits-all solution is doomed to failure if it doesn't take into account how you function?

"Your financial behavior originates in your unconscious attitudes about money," writes financial planner Brent Kessel. "Our early experiences with money cause us to cling unconsciously to specific strategies to feel secure and happy about our financial decisions. But they are not always the best options. If you want to make lasting changes in your relationship to money, you must first understand your money personality."[7]

Money mentor Vivian Baniak agrees, noting that a financial plan designed for a partner who is detail-oriented will never work if the other partner is fun-loving and unstructured.[8] However you define your personality type, trouble is inevitable if one of you expects every cent to add up accurately in your joint account and the other doesn't even remember they wrote a check.

After one too many tension-filled sessions trying to answer Jim's questions about why I had forgotten to record several checks, he came up with a solution: separate bank accounts. This might not work for every couple, but it has reduced friction in our relationship. If I fail to keep an accurate tally, I have to deal with the consequences.

To identify your personality's financial strengths and weaknesses, look over the following traits observed by Baniak.[9] Which best describes you? Which seems like your husband? Can you see why you handle money differently and possibly get upset with each other?

Sanguine. Being the fun-loving type, sanguines usually find it easy to spend on what makes them look or feel good. Prone to impulse buying, they often run up credit-card debt, forgetting to keep tabs on what they've spent. When the bills arrive, the sanguine is shocked that their bargains cost so much. For this personality type, spending relieves stress, produces happy feelings, and satisfies their need for stimulation.

Choleric. Conservative with money, the choleric keeps tight control of the household purse. They consider purchases carefully, are not inclined to impulse shopping, and don't give in easily to pleas for extra spending money unless they approve of how it is spent. With their gift for organization and drive to achieve, the choleric is able to set and meet financial goals. Being go-getters and problem solvers, they are easily frustrated by a spouse who either resists their pragmatic solutions to financial problems or procrastinates for so long nothing ever changes.

Phlegmatic. This personality type is propelled by a strong desire to avoid conflict over money. They want peace at any price. The phlegmatic avoids confrontation even when overcharged and is a soft touch when asked directly for money. They also prefer to simply pay the tab at restaurants rather than divvy it up. They are usually content with what they have materially and are disinclined to take needless financial risks. Phlegmatics are frequently what Brian Kessler describes as "the Caretaker," individuals who give generously and lend money to show compassion and support.[10]

Melancholy. The melancholy is considered the most frugal of all the personality types. Their preference is to buy items of quality that will last and never need replacing. Styles may change, family members may plead, but if that old, sturdy, ugly-but-good-quality piece of furniture might last another five years, it stays. Melancholies know what they owe because they like details, keep meticulous financial records, and can tell you exactly where every penny is spent, invested, and hidden away for that sure-to-come rainy day.

Benefit from Your Battles

As you read through these observations of different personality types, did you recognize yourself? Your husband? Your issues?

God wants you to benefit from seeing what lies behind your money battles. Pay attention to your past experiences, reflect on what money means to you, identify unresolved tensions, and notice where your personality traits affect your behavior. To begin using this information for the good of your marriage, jot down some key insights you've gained so far about yourself and your husband.

_____

_____

Because battles over finances are one of the leading causes of divorce, I encourage you to make this subject a specific focus of prayer. Using the information you've recorded above, create a personal prayer guide.

Solomon writes, "How much better to get wisdom than gold, to get insight rather than silver!" (Proverbs 16:16). When we don't see eye-to-eye, we need wisdom and understanding. Both of these qualities come from the Lord.

God's answers sometimes come in a flash of insight. More often they come as we keep praying and asking for guidance. As you seek His help to more positively handle your money differences, here are some suggestions for prayer.

- Ask God to show you what creates the most conflict between you.
- Pray for a soft spirit toward your husband and the ability to accept and work with your personality differences.
- Pray for a willing heart to see what steps He wants you to take to defuse your financial quarrels.

After you've taken time to seek the Lord, be vulnerable and talk to your husband about what you've learned. But remember, you can't change him. You can change only yourself. You have the power to alter how you manage the money you're responsible for, how you act toward your husband when you disagree, and how you view your situation. You can respond with resentment or with bold faith that the Lord will provide what you need both financially and emotionally.

As you reflect on what ignites your financial fights, choose to trust Him to work in your relationship. What you might have viewed as impossible until now—fewer fights over money and a much higher level of marital contentment—is possible. But God won't wave a magic wand. He will not do things for you that you must do. His plan and promise is to help you grow spiritually and personally as you respond to Him. Are you ready to begin?

What Is My Part in Building Our Marriage?

Start with God

If money is not simply a means to enjoy ourselves, to symbolize our success, to be our security against the unknown, or to be used as power to control others and get our way, how are we to view it? And does it matter to God?

Scripture makes it abundantly clear that how we handle the money entrusted to us matters. We aren't sole owners of all we have. To the contrary, all we have belongs to God. Recognizing this fact and acting from this conviction is the starting point for finding financial harmony.

God's Word has much to say about how we're to think about money and how we're to use it. The Old Testament talks of honesty, integrity, and fairness, giving specific instructions for ethical financial behavior. The importance of hard work versus laziness is emphasized. Principles are given for treating employees fairly, planning for the future, saving and investing, lending and giving. Those who are generous, care for the poor, look out for widows and orphans, and sacrificially meet the needs of others are esteemed by God.

In the New Testament, Jesus pointed to the powerful link between our money and our priorities: "Where your treasure is, there your heart will be also" (Matthew 6:21). Responding to a family feud over an inheritance, Jesus saw the real heart issue, uttering words that pierce even today: "Watch out! Be on your guard against all kinds of greed; life does not consist in an abundance of possessions" (Luke 12:15).

The apostle Paul urges us to free ourselves from the love of money and learn contentment. Peter exhorts against greediness. James warns against a worthless faith that feels only sympathy for those in need but doesn't follow through with action. All of Scripture affirms what Jesus declared: Our lives can possess an inner wealth, a rich satisfaction that has no connection to what we own, where we live, or how much we have stored away.

These teachings are not mere words. They are power for living an abundant life. Are they speaking to you? Will you allow them to soak into your heart?

If you're ready to move toward a new level of financial oneness with your spouse, review the following suggestions. Perhaps you are cynical due to previous attempts to find common ground, but stay expectant and hopeful. With prayers and the right attitude, you'll find ideas that will benefit your relationship.

Choose to Focus on Solutions

Get to Know Each Other

What do you know of each other's financial history? I don't mean your banking history. I mean the experiences and feelings from your background that are associated with money.

Make an agreement to set aside time to talk face-to-face. Choose a private, relaxing environment, play soft background music, and kick off your "let's get to know each other" session by discussing some non-threatening areas:

- How did your families celebrate Christmas and birthdays? Did they spend a lot for presents or parties?
- Were there family rules about what you should do with money gifts from a relative or income from a job?
- Did both your parents work outside the home?
- How did your parents handle their finances?
- What were your feelings about money once you had a job?

After you've discussed these common growing-up experiences, address the issues covered in this chapter. Talk about what money symbolizes to each of you and how your upbringings helped shape this. But be careful to notice when your husband has reached his conversational limit. Allow it to end when his eyes drift. If he looks as though he's desperate to get away, save other topics for another time.

Some couples can commit to a weekly session that stretches into the unknown future, but that isn't true for everyone. Perhaps you can shoot for every other week, or maybe you and your spouse do better with spontaneity. Go with what works for your personalities and schedules.

Remember, your goal is to get to know each other, not create another issue to argue over.

Share Your Hearts

Once you've heard each other's stories, move on to other important topics:

- What are your dreams for us financially? What kind of lifestyle do you hope we can live someday—home, vacations, funds for education, car, travel, retirement, serving the Lord?

- What does "living a rich life" mean to you, to me? Is it accumulating money, having plenty put away for that rainy day, owning certain possessions, being able to give generously?

- What do we both want our lives to be about?

Your spouse might never have thought about these issues, so don't press for answers. On the other hand, he might have a clear vision of what he wants for both of you, but he's kept it to himself. Whatever the situation, honor his input. Use this opportunity to share your dreams also.

Adopt Stay-Cool Strategies

Now that you've spent time getting to know each other on a deeper level, you're ready for the next step. But before you get down to the nitty-gritty stuff—budgets, savings, spending, and other potentially volatile topics—establish ground rules. Rather than wasting your time and leaving you more frustrated with each other than before, these stay-cool strategies will allow you both to come out as winners.

Agree to allow the other to speak without interruption.

If either of you has the tendency to jump in whenever you disagree or to start right away criticizing the other's ideas and beliefs, make a commitment to restrain yourself. For help, review the information on "the Floor" model found in chapter 8, "He Handles Conflict One Way, I Handle It Another."

Agree to respect the other's right to their views.

You might strongly disagree with your spouse's ideas and convictions, but he has a right to them. And you have a right to yours. Use this time to express curiosity rather than criticism, asking him questions to understand what he bases his views on. Share your views also, explaining why they are important to you.

Agree to treat each other as equals.

Be willing to listen to the pros and cons of the other's position. Allow both of your opinions to be heard and considered equally. If you're comfortable, pray together about your different views, either silently or out loud. Commit to being open to what God impresses on you, even if it isn't your preference.

Agree on who owns your money.

Is it God's? Does it belong to you equally? Or does the higher wage earner claim control? Research shows that when partners believe they have equal control over how money is spent, they are more satisfied with their marriage.[11]

In the interest of building harmony rather than stirring up hostility, it's important to come to an agreement that neither of you owns it all. Nor does one of you have veto power over the other or the right to single-handedly control how your money is used. This can be a difficult goal to achieve if one of you is used to making all the decisions, but prayer can move mountains or give the patience needed to live with what refuses to budge.

Agree on a Budget

There's a reason the word *budget* crops up in every discussion about money. In his book *Marriage on the Rock*, Jimmy Evans writes, "Financial counselors tell me they have never counseled a couple who have a budget for major financial problems. By budgeting, major problems are avoided."[12]

Among many benefits, having a budget reduces conflict, forces you to face financial facts, lowers fears of accumulating debt, and enables you to plan for future needs. Because so many marital fights are linked to financial issues, agreeing on a budget is essential. But there is more to designing a budget than simply agreeing on its necessity.

Quarrels can arise over what items to include. Deciding how to allocate funds can produce disagreements. You might have different ideas over how to keep track of expenses, and even who should take responsibility for making sure the system is working and bills are being paid. Be prepared to be patient with each other. Listen carefully, ask questions, and stop and pray as you tackle each step of this process.

DECIDE WHO TAKES RESPONSIBILITY.

After listening to my groans about not having much money left in our account each month, Jim presented me with a challenge: "I want you to pay the bills for three months. You need to see where it all goes so you understand I'm not hiding it from you." I never thought he was. But paying the bills opened my eyes to how much it costs to run a home. It also cured me of moaning about money.

If one of you is more financially savvy than the other, let that person pay the bills and watch over the budget. In my case, it's my husband. In your relationship, perhaps it's you. The woman described in Proverbs 31 competently handled the household money. This didn't seem to trouble her husband who was respected in the community and took pleasure in his wife, praising her capabilities (vv. 23, 28-29).

Laurie Winslow Sargent describes how she and her husband handle their budget:

> We take turns managing our finances, depending on who has time. We pay most of our bills online. For now, I manage this, so of course I see what's upcoming. This means that when my husband takes his turn, he has to remember

to look not just at our checking account balance, but also pay close attention to scheduled bills and their dates on the "Bill Pay" page. Sometimes our balance looks prettier than it actually is or will be in a week.

Sharing the responsibility works for this couple. As you work on your own budget, decide whether you'll manage it together or if one of you is better suited to the task.

MEET REGULARLY.

Many financial advisers recommend having a regular weekly meeting. This may or may not work for you, but in the interest of avoiding more conflict over money, try to pencil in at least a monthly date to review your budget.

CREATE A BUDGET THAT FITS YOUR LIFE.

Many resources are available to help you organize your budget. You can find these at your local library, a bookstore, online, or through your church. Rather than looking at this process as a painful necessity, consider that you are proactively taking charge of your money so you can put it to the best use. View it as a positive, not a negative. To kick off your new project (or to revive your previous attempts), start by keeping track of everything you've taken in and spent for a month. Then use this realistic gauge as a budget template.

IDENTIFY ITEMS YOU CONSIDER A NECESSITY.

"When Trevor saw what I paid to keep my hair colored and styled, he was shocked," said my newly married friend, Tracy. "He was even more horrified when I told him what good shoes and work clothes cost. He had no idea how much more women have to pay."

If you need a haircut every month, put the amount in the budget. All of it. Plus the tip. Discuss what's really important to add to your list of monthly expenses. Be willing to prioritize, eliminating what you can do without until your situation changes.

In our shopping-crazed culture, it's tempting to ignore the lack of available funds, pull out the credit cards, and plunge into unnecessary debt. But with God's help, you don't have to. Not having as much as you'd like and having to make hard choices is an opportunity to grow spiritually.

Before you go browsing or looking for bargains, pray. Do you really need to go—or are you putting yourself in a place of temptation? If you're serious about reducing the tension in your marriage caused by overspending, give your wants to Jesus. Ask Him to create in your heart what the apostle Paul had to learn: "the secret of being content in any and every situation" (Philippians 4:12).

INCLUDE SOME SPENDING MONEY.

Having a budget helps keep spending under control. But each spouse should have a monthly amount to spend as they wish. Be sure to come to a mutual agreement on the amount, determining together what this figure should be. In addition, set a ceiling on what either you or your husband can spend without checking in with the other.

Although cutting down on expenses is often an important part of reducing conflict, some things are worth paying for. If you're both working outside the home, consider setting aside a certain amount of money each month for meals or other services. Convenience does cost, but it also pays big dividends: less exhaustion and tension, and more energy and interest in being that warm and loving wife your husband thought he was marrying.

Money Isn't the Problem

"The love of money is a root of all kinds of evil," Paul wrote in his letter to Timothy (1 Timothy 6:10). Having money is not the problem. But loving money, fighting over it, using it selfishly, and allowing it to create hurt and even hatred are some of the evils Paul warns against. This is the opposite of what God desires.

God's desire is to bless you with a joy and confidence in Him that is far more satisfying than any earthly possession. He lovingly promises to provide all that you need, not all that you dream about.

Because God works in every situation for your good, sorting through financial differences with your husband is an opportunity for you to grow personally and spiritually. Study what the Bible has to say about money. Pray for God's perspective. Make necessary changes in your attitudes and actions, and commit to trusting God for everything you need. He is faithful to His Word and wants to guide you safely through this marital minefield. With God's help, instead of dreading the tension and explosions that money talks often produce, you can testify to His power to unite you. Then go get an ice cream and celebrate how far you've come.

May I Pray for You?

Loving Father, You who own all that exists, bless Your daughter with a heart that treasures You before any earthly object. May her mind, thoughts, and desires be fixed on things above, those joys and delights that come from a vibrant and growing relationship with You. May she trust in You with all her heart and seek Your wisdom as she addresses the difficult and divisive issue of handling finances. Give her a soft heart toward her husband, and give her husband love and understanding. Remove any anxiety and fill her heart with Your peace and assurance that You are at work on her behalf. Amen.

(ADAPTED FROM ACTS 17:24; COLOSSIANS 3:1;
PROVERBS 3:5; 1 CORINTHIANS 13; PHILIPPIANS 4:6-7)

Ten

We're Not on the Same Page Spiritually

I urge you to live a life worthy
of the calling you have received.

EPHESIANS 4:1

struggle with my young sons every Sunday because they want to stay home with their dad," said Pamela, a young mom in the Bible Study Fellowship class that I taught. "I knew Brad wasn't a believer when we got married, but I plunged ahead anyway. I really thought he'd turn to God before long so I never considered that once we had kids, his disinterest in church would affect them."

Pam was the first of many women I've listened to over the years. Tearfully pouring out their hearts, they long for their husbands to share their belief in Jesus, to attend church with the family, and to read the Bible and pray with them.

Janie, a beautiful fiftyish woman, clings to what her husband said three decades earlier. "Before we were married, I made it clear that I wouldn't marry someone who wasn't a Christian. When Blaine told me he had given his life to Christ, I was thrilled. I've gently encouraged him to attend church with me all these years, but he rarely does."

Nancy's husband, Mark, says he is a Christian, but he no longer attends church. After his former pastor implemented various changes he couldn't agree with, Mark left the church, taking Nancy with him. "I left with Mark even though I didn't agree with his position," Nancy said. "What else could I do? I miss my friends so much, and it hurts not to be with them at Bible study every week. They were my spiritual support system."

These true stories illustrate some of the struggles that occur when couples differ over spiritual issues. Perhaps you see yourself in one of them. Or maybe you're journeying through your own variation on a theme: How do I live out my faith when my partner has no interest in God? How do I get him to attend church *and* get involved? How can I encourage him to be the spiritual influence our children need? These hard questions, asked through tears or teeth gritted in frustration, are nothing new.

Women's Longings

Since the early days of the church, women have prayed for their husbands to come to Christ. If they were married to believers, they longed for them to passionately pursue God. It is no different today. We have expectations of our husbands, even if they do go to church with us.

We wonder, "What is it with men that they don't relate to God like we do? Why don't they show their feelings? How can they just stand there in church like rigid poles with their arms glued to their sides? Why don't they talk to people they don't know during the greeting time? In fact, why don't they talk to the people they do know? Why are men so strange, so unlike us?"

The questions go on.

If it's tough for women to fathom a man's response when working through day-to-day issues, it is even more complicated when it involves what men believe and how they express their faith. As a couple, you can learn practical skills that help you communicate more clearly, discover how to disagree without ushering in World War III, and find ways to rein in out-of-control spending. You can even learn how to become more attuned to your spouse's emotional needs. But how do you figure out what your husband really thinks and believes and why he acts the way he does—whether he's a Christian or not?

Once again, we find ourselves trying to decipher the male psyche.

Like other flummoxed females, we're asking the question posed throughout this book: *Why can't he be more like me?* Only this time it takes a deeper tone.

Why Can't He Be More Like Me Spiritually?

Let's find some answers, beginning with the most obvious.

He Doesn't Share Your Christian Faith

When Pam married Brad, she knew the Bible's exhortation: "Don't become partners with those who reject God. How can you make a partnership out of right and wrong? That's not partnership; that's war" (2 Corinthians 6:14 MSG).

"I was young and crazy in love with Brad," Pam explained, "so we married right after graduation from college. My parents pleaded with me not to marry an unbeliever, but I couldn't imagine not being with him and refused to break it off. Now that I'm a mom and have grown up a bit, I realize that God says this for our protection. But it's hard to obey once you've fallen in love."

Perhaps you identify. Maybe you're married to someone who doesn't share your love for Jesus. You might have plunged into marriage, like Pam, believing it would all work out. Or you became a Christian after marriage. In either case, you find yourself spiritually single, praying and pleading with God to turn your husband's heart toward Him.

Much as you might wish for a magic wand that will suddenly transform the one you love into a committed Christian, you won't find it. But you are not helpless. There is a role for you to play as you cooperate with God in discovering ways to reach your spouse. Begin by asking Him to help you discover what your husband does believe.

What Does Your Husband Believe?

If your spouse seems indifferent to issues of faith or won't talk to you about what he does believe, it doesn't mean he lacks his own ideas about why we're here and what life is all about. Whether he's shown any spiritual curiosity in the past or not, that time will come. Be assured, at some point in his life certain universal questions will crash into his mind like an unwelcome meteor from outer space.

The birth of a child, the death of a loved one, or some other momentous event might prompt him to ask: *Is there a reason I'm here? What is my purpose? Why is there suffering and evil? What happens after death?*

"Spirituality and faith are powerful and prevalent dimensions of the human experience," write the authors of *The Couple Checkup*.[1] It doesn't matter how old we are, where we live, or what work we do, at some point we all think about the unknown.

Your husband might not follow an established religion. Perhaps he subscribes to a common belief that if his good deeds outweigh his bad, he'll go to heaven. Or if he gives to charity or helps the needy, he'll earn favor with God. Of course, he might not believe in either God or heaven. Nevertheless, he still has beliefs that attempt to answer life's inevitable questions. And those beliefs govern his responses to you and your relationship.

His Early Years Shaped His Thinking

The beliefs of our family of origin are imprinted on all of us. My father repeatedly instructed my sisters and me never to date a man who didn't drink. In his perspective, a man's ability to "hold his drink" showed masculinity. He also believed that only weak and sissy men went to church.

> The beliefs of our family of
> origin are imprinted on all of us.

After I became a follower of Jesus, my father met men who caused him to reexamine his stereotypes—especially when I introduced him to my six-foot-five-inch, adventure-loving husband.

If your unbelieving spouse was raised with distorted ideas about Christianity or watched significant adults in his life scorn anything religious, his thinking is inevitably bent toward disbelief and disinterest. As you live with the results, understand that his belief system was shaped long before you married.

Dare to Have Hope

Don't despair. Your story doesn't end here. The Body of Christ is filled with men and women who grew up in families that dismissed God. Still, the Holy Spirit found, wooed, and transformed them. Put your hope in God—not in your feminine wiles, passionate pleas, or reasoned arguments. Remember that God is in the business of renewing minds. His power is not limited. He answers prayer in His sovereign timing and declares without hesitation,

> Surely the arm of the LORD is not too short to save,
>   nor his ear too dull to hear.
>   (Isaiah 59:1)

Never give up hope that one day you and your husband might know and serve the living God together.

DIG FOR UNDERSTANDING

To get a clearer understanding of where your husband stands spiritually and the extent to which his early years shaped his views, ask him. You can use the following questions to help get your discussion moving. Tell him you'd like to know more about what influenced him as a child and better understand his viewpoint.

If he isn't comfortable talking about these topics, don't press the issue. Instead, go through them yourself, looking for insights into what shaped his beliefs. If he's interested, be ready to share your own experiences.

1. Did your parents follow a religion? How did they practice it?

2. What impression did your parents' beliefs make on you?

3. Were you taken regularly to church or Sunday school? What did you like or dislike about it?

4. Did your father take an active spiritual role in your family?

5. Were there other significant people in your early years who influenced your thinking? How did they do this?

6. Have you ever had a spiritual experience or sensed God's presence? What did you make of this?

As you reflect on what you've learned from looking at each other's backgrounds, pay attention to any connections you see between his early influences and current views. Rather than poking holes in what he told you or trying to correct his opinions, pray for the ability to understand and accept the reasons for his position. You don't have to agree. Instead, pray about the insights you've gained and ask how you can use them to win his heart to the Lord.

In contrast to Pam whose husband has no desire to know God, your spouse might claim he is a believer. But he shows no interest in living as a follower of Jesus. Let's look at some possible reasons for this.

He Says He Is a Christian, But...

Janie lives with the heartache of believing that Blaine is a child of God, but he shows no desire to develop an active relationship with Christ. Blaine belongs to a vast group of men, from teenagers to seniors, who share a common experience. They once professed personal faith in the Lord but no longer follow Him. Perhaps his disinterest stems from one of the following reasons.

SPIRITUAL NEGLECT

Drifting away from the Lord is always a danger. "We must pay the most careful attention, therefore, to what we have heard, so that we do not drift away," warned the writer of Hebrews (Hebrews 2:1). He urged his readers repeatedly to pursue their relationship with God. "Let us draw near to God with a sincere heart...Let us hold unswervingly to the hope we profess...Let us consider how we may spur one another on...not giving up meeting together, as some are in the habit of doing, but encouraging one another" (Hebrews 10:22-25).

Instead of drawing near to God, your husband may have developed a habit of repeatedly ignoring His invitation to come close. With the fast-paced, demanding lives most of us live, we have to intentionally carve out time to read the Word, connect with God through prayer, and renew our spiritual passion by meeting with other believers for worship and encouragement. If we don't, we drift.

In his compilation of writings on prayer, Nick Harrison comments on this subtle but pervasive struggle that tempts all believers. "If we ignore His call to us, we will grow all the colder. Temptations are less easily overcome. Cynicism moves in, along with his twin companion, doubt. From them heartache and depression result. Don't let the apostasy begin. Stay with God."[2]

Sin Damage

Mark has been an active Christian for many years. When he found himself disagreeing with his pastor, he left the church. He had stated his views bluntly and loudly, but the pastor and leaders refused to be intimidated. Now Mark sits home nursing a bitter spirit.

After retiring from her career as a physician, the late Dorothy Ritzman decided to work as a chaplain at local nursing homes. Sharing about her work one evening, she said, "I am amazed and saddened at how many residents I come across who left churches years ago over some dispute, and they are bitter and angry to this day."

Could this be the reason your husband has lost his interest and desire for God? Has he taken offense over some issue at church or with an individual who was once a friend? Hebrews 12:15 warns, "See to it that no one falls short of the grace of God and that no bitter root grows up to cause trouble and defile many." Is your husband allowing a bitter root to grow stronger by refusing to bring it to the Cross?

No wife dares to sit in God's place and judge her husband. But in marriage, each can see the failings of the other. If your husband is refusing to deal with a sinful attitude, he might be crabby and easily upset by little things or withdrawn and absorbed in his thoughts. These are common consequences of wrestling with a conscience that refuses to repent, though the Spirit of God continues to speak.

No wife dares to sit in God's place and judge her husband.

Has some incident hurt your husband deeply? Does he need help to get past it? If so, maybe your heart aches for him and you pray constantly that he find a way to surrender his feelings and move on. On the other hand, maybe his refusal to deal with what happened makes you angry. His attitude has a negative effect on your marriage and family life, and the longer he refuses to get right with God, the more you all suffer.

If your husband is open to your input, share your concerns. Express your desire for him to be your spiritual partner once again. Support him, affirm his significance to you, and ask how you can move forward together—even if it means giving up attending a church or group that means a great deal to you. Realize you can always meet up with friends from the past, but it is your husband who will walk with you into a new future.

Church Doesn't Appeal to Him

"The average church appeals more to a woman than to a man," asserts David Murrow in his hard-hitting book, *Why Men Hate Going to Church*. Drawing on extensive research, he states, "Adult women outnumber adult men by almost two-to-one in a typical congregation."[3]

Why is this?

Although regular church attendance isn't a guarantee of personal faith, the majority of serious Christians make this a priority. If your husband doesn't claim to follow Jesus, it's understandable that he would rather stay home than attend church. However, he might surprise you, as Maxine discovered when she mentioned a specific need to her husband, Ron.

"When the church announced they needed shuttle drivers to take people from a nearby parking lot to the church each Sunday, I mentioned it to Ron," Maxine said. "He had never come to church with me before, but he was willing to help out. That was months ago. Now he comes every week and knows lots of people because they ride the shuttle. It's really neat the way the Lord got Ron into church."

If your husband does claim some sort of faith in God, perhaps he's avoiding church for a more subtle reason. Maybe he believes that a real man doesn't belong there.

"Men care about how other men view them," explained Randy Archer, a surfer, father, and pastor. "We want to succeed, to accomplish stuff, to conquer—whether it's a monster wave or racing downhill on a bike. Men like to tease and brag and get physical. They'd rather shoot hoops or do something physical than sit around sharing their emotions. It's a real turnoff when they're expected to open up. We don't like being vulnerable, which is why we keep quiet or say as little as possible in group situations."

In contrast, most women thrive in an environment where we can share life events and receive emotional support. Because of how we're made, a healthy and caring church is the ideal place for us to worship God and have our needs met.

At church, we find other women to talk to, babies to coo at, hurting friends to hug, music that produces tears, and stirring sermons that console or convict. We feel connected, useful, needed. Maybe someone asks us to serve in an area we're passionate about. Another stops us to share how much our words encouraged them. And on the way home, we bask in the joy of God's blessings, praising Him for belonging to such a spiritually rich community.

Looking at church attendance from this perspective, it's understandable that women are enthusiastic supporters and outnumber men in most places of worship.

You might not relate to what you've read so far because both you and your husband are active believers. Unlike many of your sisters in Christ who are married to men claiming no faith or who show little spiritual interest, the two of you share a relationship built on pleasing the Lord. If this is your situation, recognize what a gift you have. You are blessed.

However, as you've probably experienced, sharing a vibrant faith doesn't guarantee shared views. Differences and misunderstandings can still come between you.

We're Both Believers, But We're Not Spiritual Clones

"Jim and I visited a friend's church last week," I confided to Marilyn, breaking into a smile. "The worship leader insisted that everyone raise their hands, which is *not* Jim's style, but he had little choice. It was a small congregation so he couldn't hide behind anyone.

"I was curious about how Jim would handle this, so I glanced over at him. He had raised his hands only to his waist. He looked like some-one had pointed a gun at him and said, 'Stick 'em up.' I couldn't help myself. It cracked me up and I started laughing. Of course, he wasn't in the least bit amused, and I had to apologize afterwards."

When it comes to how we worship God, Jim and I are not spiritual clones. He was raised in a nonexpressive church, so it's natural that he is more comfortable in a traditional setting—singing hymns and fol-lowing a predictable order of service. I enjoy this too, but I come alive when the music is upbeat and I can physically express my feelings in worship.

We have learned the hard way that neither of us can change the other into our own image. We are different. And rather than argue about it, we have given each other the freedom to be who we are. I don't push Jim to act like me, and he doesn't stop me from being my more animated self. We are both followers of Jesus and that's what matters.

To gain more understanding of your spouse and yourself, let's explore two more possible reasons for not being spiritually identical. The first is your personality type, your inborn preference that deter-mines what appeals to you. In the spiritual realm this often influences the kind of worship you like or the style of sermon that grabs your attention. It also affects how you prefer to learn and deepen your faith.

The second reason for not being spiritually alike is that equally devoted Christians draw near to God through different experiences or pathways. These particular triggers turn up the heat of our passion for the Lord. And they could well be different for both of you.

What Are Your Spiritual Personalities?

In her helpful book, *Your Spiritual Personality*, Marita Littauer explains how our personality type affects how we approach our spiri-tual life. When we understand our spiritual personality, we understand our natural bent toward certain spiritual exercises.[4]

Remembering this principle can prevent hours of fuming and fuss-ing when your husband doesn't want to go to an event you are dying to attend. If you want to do something badly enough, go with friends or by yourself. Then come home and tell him all about it.

To discover your spiritual personalities, check which of the following statements best describes each of you. Is one of you more sanguine, choleric, melancholy, or phlegmatic than the other? Invite your husband to take this quiz so he can identify where he sees himself. If he's reluctant, do it for him to the best of your ability. Then repeat the exercise with yourself in mind.

	My husband	*Me*	*Both of us*
Are You a Sanguine?			
You enjoy greeting visitors at church.	❏	❏	❏
You like being part of a group project.	❏	❏	❏
You prefer how-to sermons.	❏	❏	❏
You're expressive and share easily.	❏	❏	❏
You grow best by being with others.	❏	❏	❏
Are You a Choleric?			
You see needs and know how to meet them.	❏	❏	❏
You initiate new ministries.	❏	❏	❏
You enjoy leading committees and groups.	❏	❏	❏
You relate to sermons that challenge you.	❏	❏	❏
You get frustrated with the status quo.	❏	❏	❏
Are You a Melancholy?			
You like to sit and talk to God, content in His presence.	❏	❏	❏
You're a learner—studying Scripture is deeply satisfying.	❏	❏	❏
Your goals reflect eternal values.	❏	❏	❏
You love theological sermons explaining key doctrines.	❏	❏	❏
You try to avoid group activities that seem superficial.	❏	❏	❏

	My husband	Me	Both of us

Are You a Phlegmatic?

	My husband	Me	Both of us
You prefer to wait until asked to get involved.	❑	❑	❑
You expect the service to begin and end on time.	❑	❑	❑
You don't identify or express your feelings easily.	❑	❑	❑
You avoid loud groups that like to debate issues.	❑	❑	❑
You enjoy a regular time of spiritual devotions.	❑	❑	❑

How would you describe your spiritual personality? Can you identify what kind of church culture or Christian practices help you thrive? Are they the same or different for your husband? Rather than allowing these insights to divide you spiritually, see them as an opportunity to continue maturing and working out your faith in real-life situations.

If you don't approach God the same way or find yourselves attracted to the same activities, look for solutions. Be willing to flex with each other and pray for creative ways to handle issues that currently create tension. Asking God to give you soft and obedient hearts is essential. So is being willing to practice what Scripture says: "Do nothing out of selfish ambition or vain conceit. Rather, in humility value others above yourselves, not looking to your own interests but each of you to the interests of the others" (Philippians 2:3-4).

What Pathways Point You to God?

In his enlightening book, *Sacred Pathways,* Gary Thomas details a variety of ways that draw us into God's presence: "He created you with a certain personality and a certain spiritual temperament. God wants your worship, according to the way he made you."[5]

In this chapter we've looked at many reasons why your spouse isn't more like you spiritually. But there is another, easily forgotten factor to consider. God is behind your unique design. He made you different, even to the extent of what resonates within your spirit and most deeply attracts you to Him.

God made you different, even to the
extent of what resonates within your spirit
and most deeply attracts you to Him.

Bearing these truths in mind, look over the following descriptions of different pathways into God's presence. Which ones resonate with you? Can you tell which resonate with your husband?

Naturalists delight in God's presence when out of doors. They love camping, hiking, climbing mountains, watching waves crash, and reveling in the power and majesty of God, the Creator.

Sensates revel in loving God through all their senses: seeing, hearing, smelling, tasting, touching. Their spirits are overwhelmed by the unseen God who dwells in light unapproachable.

Traditionalists sense God best when observing rituals, meditating on Scripture, and incorporating symbols into their worship of the eternal God.

Ascetics feel closest to God in solitude and simplicity. Spending time in silence, fasting, and acts of service are ways they express their devotion to Christ, the One who gave Himself for them.

Activists show their devotion to God through confronting injustice and evil. They cannot help speaking up when they see wrong tolerated, whether in the church or the community.

Caregivers worship God by compassionately caring for others. They express their devotion to Christ as they sacrificially yet joyfully meet the needs of the sick, the lonely, the hungry, and the destitute.

Enthusiasts rejoice in God with exuberance. They delight in mystical experiences of His reality: exciting answers to prayer, being overwhelmed by His presence in worship, and expecting Him to move in supernatural ways.

Contemplatives crave time to adore God. They hunger for intimacy with Him and their delight comes from resting in His presence, caught up in the wonder of His glory.

Intellectuals experience God as they fill their minds with His Word and other inspirational books. They are stimulated by understanding new concepts about Him that open up their hearts.

Can you recall situations or experiences that produced in you a powerful sense of God's reality and presence? What about your husband?

One of you might feel closest to God when you're sitting alone on a mountaintop contemplating creation. Or you're most alive when serving on the worship team. Spending time in Scripture, searching out the root meanings of Greek verbs might thrill you. Whichever pathway leads you to express your desire for God, rejoice in it. Act on it. Be energized by it.

And allow your husband the freedom to respond to God in the unique way that stirs his soul.

What Is My Part in Building Our Marriage?

Let's be honest. We want our husbands to be a clone of Jesus. Perfect. Holy. Without a shred of selfishness in their bones. We want a man who overflows with love, who is always compassionate, and who is sensitive to our needs. One who is wise in his counsel, who knows exactly what words encourage us, and who knows when to say nothing more.

> Let's be honest. We want our husbands
> to be a clone of Jesus. Perfect. Holy. Without
> a shred of selfishness in their bones.

What Christian woman wouldn't want a man who rises early for time with God? A mate who gathers you and the children around the table every evening and reads the Word—explaining it with humor, stories, and real-life, age-appropriate applications? One who prays sincere, Spirit-anointed requests? Just "Give us Jesus" is our cry!

But that's not going to happen.

God has given you a flesh-and-blood male. One who has passions, problems, and a personality that challenges *you* to grow more like Jesus. Are you ready to do this? Or are you tempted to retort, "Well what about him? He's the one causing the problems. He needs to grow."

I hear you. I understand. But you can't make him change.

What you can do is make it your ambition to become the best wife you can be. And Scripture is full of practical insights to help you achieve this goal.

Wordless Power

In a portion of his first letter written to the early Christians, the apostle Peter specifically addresses women who are married to unbelievers. What he says applies to every wife who longs to be a spiritual influence on her husband. How you treat your husband, what you say to him, and your attitude toward him at home and in public affects his openness to the gospel.

> How you treat your husband, what you say to him, and your attitude toward him at home and in public, affects his openness to the gospel.

Eugene Peterson paraphrases Peter's words this way: "Be good wives to your husbands, responsive to their needs. There are husbands who, indifferent as they are to any words about God, will be captivated by your life of holy beauty" (1 Peter 3:1-2 MSG). In other words, the way a godly, believing wife treats her husband has inherent power—so much so that she can either draw him toward the Lord or turn him away.

Speaking as a wise and Spirit-filled man, Peter explains a very important truth: Men are more receptive when their wives are loving, kind, and easy to get along with. Instead of nagging and arguing, zip your lips. Instead of negative, resentful responses because your husband doesn't share your convictions or express any interest in your beliefs, live out your character-changing faith in front of him.

Do you want to build your marriage? As a believer in Christ, indwelt by His Spirit, He has given you all you need to live "a godly life" (2 Peter 1:3). Ask God to show you what steps to take. Accept what He brings to mind. Then respond—in His power.

Be encouraged. Though your words may never open your husband's heart to the Lord, the life you live brings the power of the Holy Spirit into your home.

May I Pray for You?

Father God, please pour out Your favor on my sister who longs to live a life that pleases You. If her spouse scorns her faith or is hard and indifferent to the gospel, encourage her. As the God of all comfort, may she feel Your loving presence when she suffers for her faith. Give her wisdom to know how to live in a way that wins her husband to You. May she rely on You. Set her hope on You. And never lose heart that You are the God who gives sight to the blind. Help her to fix her eyes not on what is seen, thinking that nothing will ever change. Instead, enable her to fix her eyes on what is yet unseen. Give her the confident faith that knows You will work in her marriage as she continues to walk with You.

(ADAPTED FROM 2 CORINTHIANS 1:3-10;
PROVERBS 31:10-31; 2 CORINTHIANS 4:16-18)

Eleven

We Get "Headaches" for Different Reasons

That is why a man leaves his father
and mother and is united to his wife,
and they become one flesh.

GENESIS 2:24

While on a trip many years ago, Jim bought me a special gift. He took his time, choosing it carefully and considering what would bring me the most pleasure. When he presented me with a large, glossy shopping bag, I excitedly ripped off the tissue paper, fully expecting a special piece of lacy, racy lingerie. But it bore no resemblance to my fantasies.

My gift? A daffodil yellow, all-in-one, fleece bunny outfit. Its only decoration was a white pom-pom firmly attached to its behind.

"You're always saying how cold you feel at night, so I tried to find something that would keep you warm," Jim said. "Don't you like it?"

To be fair, I must acknowledge that despite his embarrassment, my husband has occasionally walked into shops filled with frilly feminine underwear, grabbed the first thing he saw, and hustled out as fast as he could. Perhaps that's how I ended up with something that has probably never starred in any woman's fantasies. Unless her daydreams include romantic escapades in Siberia.

Although I thanked Jim for his thoughtfulness, I never did wear my yellow bunny costume. But all was not lost. Malaika, our teenage daughter, loved having a portable blanket to snuggle in whenever the wind howled and the windows rattled on stormy winter nights.

Having Fun Is God's Idea

Have you ever wondered why sex is fundamental to a healthy marriage? Or why God encourages husbands and wives to get naked, not be ashamed of their bodies, and to actually enjoy sexual intercourse? If you're blushing at such "tell it like it is" language, let me assure you every statement is in God's Word. Check it out:

> That is why a man leaves his father and mother and is united to his wife, and they become one flesh. Adam and his wife were both naked, and they felt no shame (Genesis 2:24-25).

> May your fountain be blessed,
>   and may you rejoice in the wife of your youth.
> A loving doe, a graceful deer—
>   may her breasts satisfy you always,
>   may you ever be intoxicated with her love.
>   (Proverbs 5:18-19)

> My lover is radiant and ruddy...His lips are like lilies...His arms are rods of gold...His body is like polished ivory... His legs are pillars of marble...His mouth is sweetness itself; he is altogether lovely. This is my beloved, this is my friend (Song of Songs 5:10-16).

God isn't embarrassed by the reality of sexual desire. He created it. Nor does God keep quiet about it. The importance of being sexually available to one another within marriage is part of His design. Led by God's Spirit, the apostle Paul also addressed this subject without embarrassment. "The husband should fulfill his marital duty to his wife, and likewise the wife to her husband...Do not deprive each other except perhaps by mutual consent and for a time" (1 Corinthians 7:3,5).

"Regardless of your station or status in life," writes Gary Thomas, author of *Sacred Marriage*, "you're celebrating a deeply human dance, a transcendent experience created by no less a preeminent mind than that of Almighty God himself."[1]

People who think that God disapproves of sexual activity within marriage, or that it is somehow an occasionally necessary but shameful act, don't know their Bibles. Scripture actually *emphasizes* the key role that sex plays in creating and sustaining a strong and satisfying marriage. "Honor marriage, and guard the sacredness of sexual intimacy between wife and husband" (Hebrews 13:4 MSG).

Here are five reasons why sex with your spouse is designed to be one of God's great blessings:

1. IT GIVES PHYSICAL PLEASURE AND PRODUCES BABIES.

If the nerve endings involved in sex were anything like the nerve endings the dentist hits, very few little clones would be running around. God made our bodies to enjoy the process. He approves of physical pleasure. And babies.

2. IT SATISFIES YOUR SEXUAL HUNGER.

Like a raging river that overflows its banks and causes untold damage, uncontrolled sexual cravings devastate lives. The marriage bed is God's safe place for meeting this human desire.

3. IT MEETS YOUR NEED FOR INTIMACY.

We have a built-in longing for connection. God recognized this need in Adam and intentionally designed a woman to be his partner through life, easing the loneliness that can creep like a gray fog into the human soul (Genesis 2:18). Intimacy involves the mixing and mingling of lives and thoughts, experiences and dreams, fears and joys. The more you share of yourselves, the closer you feel to one another.

4. IT DEEPENS YOUR COMMITMENT TO EACH OTHER.

Sexual intimacy works like powerful glue bonding you together on a heart level. In *Hooked*, Drs. Joe McIlhaney, Jr. and Freda McKissic Bush state: "When two people touch each other in a warm, meaningful and intimate way, oxytocin is released. The oxytocin then does two things: increases a woman's desire for more touching and causes bonding of the woman to the man she has been spending time with in physical contact."[2] By God's design, lovemaking chemically ignites and strengthens commitment to your mate. It also draws you closer emotionally, producing tender concern for one another.

5. IT INCREASES THE JOY IN YOUR MARRIAGE.

Pleasure in bed is not limited to the physical. Enjoying each other's personality, humor, even silly antics are all ways to strengthen your relationship. Being playful in bed heightens the enjoyment factor. A smart husband with sex on his mind also knows that spending time listening to his wife and helping her with even one simple task pays dividends. On your part, offering sweet words, smiles, and a quick cuddle helps build a sense of anticipation that promises greater pleasure to follow at the right time.

These are only five of the many benefits that come from a good sex life. Stop and reflect on your relationship. Can you identify ways in which it has been strengthened by coming together sexually?

_____

_____

If your sex life is generally struggle-free, consider yourself fortunate. Even if your husband baffles or irritates you at times, a loving and considerate partner is something to celebrate.

But perhaps you're one of those women who don't feel fortunate. Maybe you wrestle with discouragement or even anger when you think about your sexual relationship. What you live with bears little resemblance to the blessings God intended. Your heart hurts. You wonder why sexual intimacy remains elusive. And you long to know what you can do to turn things around.

We'll get to those suggestions later in the chapter. First, let's explore the many reasons why the marital bed can be a source of frustration. But let me remind you that I am not a licensed counselor. Nor am I a sex therapist.

If serious sexual struggles in your marriage threaten your commitment to your spouse, cause you to sink into depression, or lead to thoughts of an emotional or physical affair, pay attention. If you sense your husband is wrestling with sexual disappointment and frustration, pay attention. These are red flags. Dismissing your difficulties in this area, or considering them inconsequential, is dangerous to any marriage.

Sex in Real Life

Sex in real life does not mimic the movies. It doesn't mirror erotic novels where the main characters meet, lock eyes, and before the evening is over are having passionate sex. It isn't a constant rerun of your favorite romantic fantasies. And it pales in comparison to the sexcapades that entice men and women to watch pornography.

Sex in real life comes packaged in a relationship between two imperfect human beings who unconsciously carry their desires, assumptions, and expectations right into the marital bed. And therein lies the source of many sexual struggles.

> Sex in real life comes packaged in a relationship between two imperfect human beings who unconsciously carry their desires, assumptions, and expectations right into the marital bed.

But don't give up. Like the other issues in marriage that make you wonder, *Why can't he be more like me?* there is hope. Struggles between you can give way to sensitivity and concern for each other. Demands that focus on either one of you getting what you want when you want it can be changed into serving the needs of the other. In God's design, the sexual relationship between a husband and wife can be spiritually transformative: a place for growing in grace, understanding, forgiveness, and unselfishness.

Before you can grow, however, you need to know what causes those headaches.

What Causes Headaches?

(Yes, men get them too.)

The No-Sex, Low-Sex Marriage

Susie wept as she shared the pain and frustration she experienced in her marriage to John:

> We became Christians in our late teens and married a year later. John worked for a local company, and I stayed home with our two little ones. We enjoyed our small church and were flattered when the leaders asked if we'd help out. We both jumped at the invitation.
>
> I'm sure everyone saw us as a normal, young Christian couple coping with the usual ups and downs of life. What they didn't know was what was going on in our sexual relationship. John had absolutely no desire for me.
>
> I would reach out to him when we went to bed, but he would turn away. I tried talking to him to find out what was wrong, but he wouldn't answer. I showered, smoothed scented lotion all over me, and wore sexy outfits to bed. But it didn't make any difference.
>
> I had put on weight, so I asked him if that was the problem. He said it wasn't. Was he no longer physically attracted to me? He shrugged his shoulders. I joined a gym, trying to lose weight. I even confided in one of the more mature women at my church. Nothing she suggested and nothing I did changed the situation.
>
> In the end I became so depressed and felt so unwanted that I filed for divorce. I know our friends at church disapproved, but I just couldn't cope emotionally with John's complete disregard for my feelings, or my need to be loved sexually.

Sadly, Susie's story is not uncommon.

Forget Stereotypes

According to marriage therapist Michele Weiner-Davis, "It is estimated that 1 out of 3 couples struggle with problems associated with low sexual desire. One study found that 20% of married couples have sex less than 10 times a year! Complaints about low desire are the #1 problem brought to sex therapists."[3]

Clearly, the stereotype that all men are sex machines with a permanent "on" button and that most women are dead from the neck down is not supported by the facts.

Carol, a mother of three single, twentysomething sons, commented on what her middle son had recently shared with her: "Jake is a good-looking guy. He's friendly and funny and people like him. Over coffee the other day he told me that the single women in his workplace come on to him, talk openly about sex, and expect it on the first date."

Sexual expectations are not limited to singles. Moms on the run, married women in the workplace, old and young, have all been affected by our self-focused culture that tells women they can and should have it all. In this case, a sensitive, romantic husband who is ready for sex whenever they are.

But as Susie discovered, not all men are ready at a moment's notice. Some struggle with low libido and don't know why or what to do about it. Others wrestle with lingering shame from past sexual experiences or childhood abuse that inhibits their desire.

Whatever the cause, in our hypersexualized culture, not wanting sex or being unable to perform erodes a man's sense of masculinity. Understandably, most men don't want to talk about this, even if their wives are sympathetic and open to finding solutions.

Perhaps you are baffled and hurt by your husband's disinterest. You want a lover, not merely a friend. You want to be touched. You long for a husband in the full sense of the word.

Or maybe you hold back, and your husband feels sex-starved. Whatever the case, a persistent refusal on either part to engage in sexual intimacy can cause a marriage to collapse.

Avoiding the topic, refusing to discuss it, or minimizing its significance will not solve the problem. If either of you struggle with low libido, it is vital to ask your spouse how your lack of intimacy affects him. Then share how it affects you. Pray for the right timing and words.

Pray for honesty and the ability to describe your struggles with compassion rather than criticism and blame.

Discuss the importance of seeking medical help for the sake of improving or even saving your marriage. If nothing is physically wrong with either of you, then make an appointment with a competent counselor who shares your Christian values. Encourage your husband to go with you. But if he won't, don't give up. Go by yourself.

The Pornography Plague

Involvement in pornography is another contributing factor to a low-sex, no-sex marriage. In an article dated March 31, 2010, National Public Radio described the addictive power of pornography.

> Imagine a drug so powerful it can destroy a family simply by distorting a man's perception of his wife. Picture an addiction so lethal it has the potential to render an entire generation incapable of forming lasting marriages and so widespread that it produces more annual revenue—$97 billion worldwide in 2006—than all of the leading technology companies combined...
>
> According to an online statistics firm, an estimated 40 million people use this drug on a regular basis...Neurological data suggest its effects on the brain are strikingly similar to those of synthetic drugs. Indeed, two authorities on the neurochemistry of addiction, Harvey Milkman and Stanley Sunderwirth, claim it is the ability of this drug to influence all three pleasure systems in the brain—arousal, satiation, and fantasy—that makes it "the piece de resistance among the addictions."[4]

Like any addiction, the more pornography is absorbed, the greater the need for more stimulation in order to achieve a high. This can lead to demands from the addicted person that their spouse dress or act like a porn star. It can also lead to humiliating comparisons and rejection.

Pornography has many victims: the spouse who is accepted or rejected based on her body or who feels she must participate in emotionally offensive sexual acts; the spouse whose mind becomes corrupted and enslaved; the children who witness their parents growing apart. And the ultimate victim is the loving relationship that God intended for a husband and wife.

As followers of a holy God who hates sin, we are called to flee evil desires, practice self-control, and live a life that pleases the Lord. If pornography is present in your marriage, don't keep it a secret. It is not God's will for you to accept or condone this addiction.

Seeking help for your marriage is a sign of strength, not weakness. The Bible tells us to pursue insight.

> The beginning of wisdom is this: Get wisdom.
> Though it cost you all you have, get understanding.
> (Proverbs 4:7)

Knowledgeable, professional counsel is an avenue through which God can help you and your spouse experience the blessings He intended.

Low libido and pornography are two of the major causes of male "headaches." Now let's turn our attention to other reasons for "headaches" that predominantly, though not exclusively, affect women.

You Want Some Romance

Are you a true romantic whose ideal sexual relationship begins early in the day? You want your husband to catch your eye at breakfast and give you that special knowing smile. Or at least, squeeze you tight while giving you more than his usual perfunctory kiss as he heads for the door. If none of these messages are downloaded into your brain at some point before "the event," you get a "headache."

Your love-pump needs priming and you wish your husband would notice and do something about it. If you could just get a little attention, affection, or verbal affirmation before heading to the bedroom, you'd be hot and raring to go. Instead, you stay frozen and frustrated in the "off" position.

How would you rate this issue in your relationship?

❑ Not a problem   ❑ Sometimes a problem   ❑ A real problem

You're Exhausted

"Jamie is very sympathetic when I plead a headache," Sophie confessed. "He knows I'm exhausted after a day taking care of our two-year-old and our new baby. But I can tell he's starting to get a little frustrated with always being last in line for my attention."

Whether you arrive home from work with bags of groceries and a family crying "What's for dinner?" or you've been home all day answering nonstop cries, it's understandable that you have zero energy to meet one more need. In our fast-paced lifestyle, exhaustion is a leading cause of nighttime headaches.

Even if your husband is kind and understanding about how hard you work, keep in mind that repeatedly saying no can create a dangerous chasm between you. After a time, it will be hard for him not to feel unwanted as a man.

Hurting from one too many rebuffs or assuming you no longer have any sexual desire for him, he is vulnerable. In his human need for connection and feeling valued, he might bury himself in work, spend extra time with friends, or even pour himself into ministry opportunities. He could also find himself susceptible to another woman who appreciates his good qualities.

How would you rate this issue in your marriage?

❏ Not a problem   ❏ Sometimes a problem   ❏ A real problem

You've Got Too Much to Do

When you feel stressed or pressured about how much you have to get done, you develop a sudden, horrendous headache. Hopping into the sack for a little pleasurable reenergizing can happen only when your tasks are finished. And there is always more to do: check a report for work, tackle another load of laundry, or answer ten more emails.

According to sex therapist Ian Kerner, "The parts of the brain associated with stress need to deactivate in order for women to focus on sex."[5] Deactivating takes more than a few minutes. It takes a few hours. Make the choice to put work aside. Intentionally stop pushing yourself to conquer another task. Relax and imagine yourself having warm, satisfying sex with your husband. By doing this, you allow your body to get ready for something far more important than checking another item off your to-do list.

How would you rate this issue in your marriage?

❏ Not a problem   ❏ Sometimes a problem   ❏ A real problem

You're Angry and Hurt

"I couldn't believe that Cliff wanted sex after we blew up at each other the other night," Tiffany said. "What is it with men that they can have sex regardless of their emotions? We've always had a rocky marriage, but we usually make up and smooth things over after a few days. I like sex, but it's hard for me to feel any desire when my feelings are hurt or I'm still mad at Cliff."

Unlike men, who can compartmentalize their emotions and have sex even if there are unresolved issues, women aren't wired to get passionate after a spat. If he apologizes, yes. But if he doesn't, he's out in the cold.

Addressing a man's capacity to have sex after a heated argument, Les Parrott, coauthor of *Saving Your Marriage Before It Starts*, says, "It's a way for him to show he still cares for you despite the fight."[6]

That's not a rationale most women get!

Persistent disinterest and refusal to have sex with your husband, however, can be due to a deeper vein of unmined resentments. Paul counsels, "Do not let the sun go down while you are still angry" (Ephesians 4:26). Instead of allowing past clashes to block the loving feelings you once had for your spouse, God says admit your anger, acknowledge how you honestly feel, and work toward resolution.

If you know your headaches are linked to repressed or barely suppressed anger, don't waste your energy hoarding grudges. Expend it on healing. Go back and read the chapters on communication and conflict. Then take whatever action you sense the Holy Spirit impressing on you.

How would you rate this issue in your marriage?

❏ Not a problem   ❏ Sometimes a problem   ❏ A real problem

You're in a Power Struggle

Having sex can be used as a bargaining chip in a battle of wills. You want something from your husband and give him a choice: either he coughs up or there's no fun in bed. He might do the same.

"I longed to be held and loved," Pauline said, "but unless I agreed to do something Eric wanted, whether in bed or out, he refused to make love. It was like making love was a treat he'd hand out if I was a good little girl. No matter how much I pleaded and argued with him that this wasn't right, he refused to be intimate with me."

Sexual intimacy becomes a power play. One of you wants affection, but the other refuses to cooperate unless his or her conditions are met. Whether it's losing fifty pounds, buying a new car, going on a fancy vacation, or giving way in some decision, using sex as a bargaining chip degrades the very core of a relationship. Becoming one physically and emotionally is intended to knit a couple together, not give one power to control the other.

How would you rate this issue in your marriage?

❏ Not a problem   ❏ Sometimes a problem   ❏ A real problem

You Have Painful Sexual Memories

If you were sexually abused as a child, the memories and feelings that flood you when your husband wants sex can quickly shut down any desire on your part. Your headaches have taproots that reach deep into your past, and even deeper into your soul. Theologian and author Steven R. Tracy writes,

> Sexual relations with even a loving husband can be a trauma trigger that evokes memories and sensations of childhood abuse. Any number of marital behaviors or experiences, from a hug in the middle of the night to the actual position of intercourse, can trigger childhood sexual trauma. Also, since sexual abuse creates distrust, the most intimate physical act—sex—often is simply too intimate to be enjoyed. Additionally, a female sexual abuse victim often develops great dissatisfaction about and even antipathy toward her

body and its sexual urges. Her abuser's interest in her body had been the source of great pain, so subconsciously her body has become the enemy.[7]

Perhaps you identify with what you've just read. If you do, my heart aches for you. I am privileged to know several women who came from sexually abusive childhoods, but over time and with the right help, the Lord set them free from their bondage to the past. This is the Lord's desire for you, my friend, but *you* must take some steps that require determination and courage.

First, pray that God will lead you to a wise, compassionate, and knowledgeable Christian counselor. Pray also for a mature and loving friend to walk through the healing journey with you. It might seem unthinkable to share your story with anyone, but God can provide the support and acceptance you need if you ask Him.

I also encourage you to read Dr. Tracy's book, *Mending the Soul,* and Stephen Viars's *Putting Your Past in Its Place.* You can experience freedom from the shame and emotional damage you suffered. And your marriage will be blessed because of your courageous refusal to let what happened in your past rob you of the joy that lies ahead.

Headaches Have Multiple Causes

This chapter cannot cover the great variety of reasons for headaches, but here are a few more you might recognize:

- You struggle with a negative body image. You'd rather avoid sex with your husband than have him see any imperfections.

- Your spouse no longer physically appeals to you, so you let your imagination dwell on a friend's husband or a new man at work.

- You feel unappreciated, put down, dominated. This has squelched your desire to make love.

- You find yourself clicking emotionally with another man. You enjoy his personality—and find your husband difficult and unpleasant to be around.

- You're bored with the same old sex scene and long for more excitement between you.

If sexual intimacy is a struggle in your marriage, take a moment and think about why. Can you pinpoint some reasons, perhaps even ones that I haven't mentioned? Make a note of what comes to mind:

_____

_____

Now clarify your desires. Ask yourself:

What would I like to see changed? _____

_____

Is what I want realistic? What are the obstacles? _____

_____

Is it an action my husband can take? What is it? _____

_____

What is in my power to change? _____

_____

What Is My Part in Building Our Marriage?

In her highly practical guide for couples, Sandra Gray Bender states a truth most wives have experienced, but wish weren't true: "Romantic love emanates from the idealization of the other person. It is a hypnotic state of mind in which positive aspects of the beloved person are affirmed and negative aspects are denied...Romantic love changes after you have been married for a while. Real life intrudes on the dream of the ideal."[8]

How true! But all is not lost. You are not doomed to live without any romance in your life. It will, however, take thought, prayer, and action on your part to "get back that lovin' feeling."

As a first step, think about when you last experienced those fizzy feelings of attraction toward your husband. What was going on when you felt this way? Consider your early days of dating and marriage. What created thrills between you? What made you delight in each other's company? What activities did you enjoy together? What commitments did you share?

Now ask yourself, *Is there anything to stop us from re-creating some of those experiences?* Your reaction might well be, *We don't have the time, energy, money, freedom, or even the desire to get romantic. Things are different now and we can't re-create the past.*

If that's your response, would you rather settle for what is? Or reach out, with God's help, for what could be?

Passion Igniters

God wants your marriage to be a blessing—to you, your spouse, your family, your church, and your community. For this to happen, it's essential that you build and maintain a sense of closeness and enjoyment of one another. Likewise, it's essential that you keep the sexual sizzle in your relationship. Here are some passion igniters that will help you accomplish both goals.

Make time for him.

Your career, family, friends, workouts, social media, even the dog, can all come ahead of dedicated time with your husband. You have to work at making your sexual relationship a priority. Arrange some "just us" time by marking your calendar for a monthly getaway from whatever keeps you occupied—and plan to be occupied with each other. Exchange child care if possible and bless another couple who needs this time as much as you two do.

Focus on being friends.

Do you remember doing fun things together? Feeling excited about your next date? Being thrilled at the thought of living together forever? Unfortunately, that level of enjoyable friendship gets lost when your emotional and physical connection is swallowed up in the routine of daily life. Friendship with your spouse needs nurturing, which requires intentional attention. To rebuild your emotional connection, share what's on your mind, discuss what happened during your day, talk about interesting items in the news, upcoming events you might attend, even cartoons or jokes that make you laugh. In a marriage, continued silence is not golden!

CHANGE YOUR MENTAL TAPES ABOUT SEX.

Don't reject your husband's desire for sex because you're "not in the mood." Instead, allow him to touch you. People experience desire differently. As you open yourself to the process of arousal, it might trigger your body's nerve endings to react with pleasure, which may prompt you to say, "Let's keep going." Loving your husband not only in word but in deed means being willing to have sex, even initiating it, and expressing your enjoyment of him as your partner. This might require rethinking your views of sexual intimacy and the part that God wants you to play in the marriage bed.

CREATE A SEXY ATMOSPHERE.

We've been created with senses that respond to appealing fragrances, warm silky skin, quiet music, flickering candles, and sensuous clothing worn strictly for his eyes only. As you make yourself and your bedroom appeal to your husband's senses, you not only honor him as your partner, you also heighten his sense of being desired by you. Be creative and think about what would appeal to him. Begin by tossing out those shapeless sweats and T-shirts, grab something feminine and slinky, and prepare to fire up your love life.

Serve Your Spouse and Grow!

In discussing the link between spiritual growth and sexuality, Gary Thomas writes, "Learning to give sexually instead of take, learning to lessen your own demands and to be more sensitive to your spouse's demands—these small choices will reap big dividends in your spiritual life because they are teaching you to become more selfless. You are imitating Jesus Christ and taking on the nature of a servant, which is your calling as a Christian."[9]

In addition to serving your husband by giving him physical pleasure and fulfillment, the sexual act expresses love, commitment, and caring. It says, "You matter to me. I accept you physically. As your wife, I consciously give my body to you in the most complete way possible that we might be one flesh." In this way, you honor the One who created you both in intricate detail—male and female. And every time you come together sexually without resenting your husband or making him think he's being a nuisance, you honor God.

As a Christian wife, you reveal your love for Jesus by doing what He asks, even in this most intimate area of your life. Whatever the struggles you are working to resolve, know that God will bless you for choosing to become a woman who blesses her husband.

May I Pray for You?

Heavenly Father, You are the One who created us male and female. Sexual desire and expression are part of Your design, not only to produce children but also to give love and pleasure to our spouse. I praise You that we are fearfully and wonderfully made. I pray for my sister, whether she longs for physical love from her husband or feels selfishly used in the marriage bed. Comfort her, Lord. Give her wisdom. Direct her prayers and her paths toward healing and hope. Show her what to do. And if she hears Your voice prompting some change on her part, I ask that Your Spirit would powerfully draw her to being willing to serve her husband, to highly esteem him, and to be a blessing to him. Amen.

(ADAPTED FROM GENESIS 1:27-28; PSALM 139:14;
JOHN 14:15,23; EPHESIANS 5:1-2)

PART 3

Where Do
I Go from Here?

Twelve

Choose to Thrive

"The joy of the LORD is your strength."

NEHEMIAH 8:10

G od is the happiest Person in the universe," declares John Johnson, a pastor and seminary professor in Portland, Oregon. "He delights in us, His creation. And having joy in Him, no matter our circumstances, is what delights God."

Held in captivity for many years, the Israelites wept when they heard God's Word taught in Jerusalem once again. They grieved over the sin that had led to their exile. But Nehemiah pointed them to another response. "Do not grieve," he said, "for the joy of the LORD is your strength" (Nehemiah 8:10). Nehemiah knew that the joy of the Lord provides supernatural strength to cope with every difficult circumstance.

Paul and Silas acted on this same spiritual truth. When they found themselves falsely accused, beaten, and imprisoned in a dark, dank dungeon, they sang and praised God (Acts 16:16-40). How could they do this? What gave them the inner stability to overcome their miserable circumstances and thrive spiritually and emotionally?

They fixed their minds on God. They believed He was with them, and they reminded themselves of His faithfulness by praying, praising, and singing spiritual songs. The result? Abundant joy and anxiety-conquering peace.

Remembering What We Know

You might know these truths for conquering discouragement, as I do. But let's be honest. Being joyful isn't always easy. Our tendency is to forget in our dark places the spiritual principles we learned in the light.

> Being joyful isn't always easy. Our tendency is to forget in our dark places the spiritual principles we learned in the light.

Wide awake in the early hours one morning, I fought a creeping sense of discouragement. My mind churned, rehearsing everything that had upset me the day before. "Lord, I need You," I whispered. "Please help me persevere."

God's voice broke through as clearly as if He had spoken audibly: "Poppy, choose to be happy. Change your perspective. I have given you the power to see life differently." His words reminded me of my long-ago prayer, "Lord, help me make my marriage as happy as possible given the enormous differences between us."

Being willing to stay in your marriage and to work on it is a choice you make. It is a commitment you make to the Lord. This doesn't guarantee you won't experience times of distress. What it does provide is an anchor to hold you steady when the storms hit and you're tempted to jump ship.

> Being willing to stay in your marriage and to work on it is a choice you make. It is a commitment you make to the Lord.

Like the Israelites in Jerusalem and Paul and Silas in Philippi, God calls us to fix our eyes on Him when life is difficult. This requires making new choices.

Choose a New Perspective

Before our hamster mysteriously disappeared, never to be seen again, I watched him running on the wheel in his cage as fast as his little legs could carry him. I marveled at how stupid he was. After all, he wasn't going anywhere. He wasn't achieving anything. His circumstances weren't changing. Perhaps he felt better in some way, but he was simply wearing himself out.

And then I saw the parallels. It isn't just hamsters who wear themselves out going nowhere.

If this is where you are, running in place emotionally and accomplishing nothing, my heart goes out to you. I have been there and I understand. But that is not where the Lord wants you to stay.

In answer to my desperate prayers as a young wife, the Lord impressed two thoughts on my heart. To have a happier marriage, I needed to make a couple of intentional choices:

1. Stop endlessly rehashing all that is negative and discouraging.

2. Choose to thrive as a woman and a child of God.

One focus drains the happiness out of our lives; the other energizes, freeing our hearts to soar with renewed strength.

> Those who hope in the LORD
>   will renew their strength.
> They will soar on wings like eagles;
>   they will run and not grow weary,
>   they will walk and not be faint.
>   (Isaiah 40:31)

God has given you the power to thrive spiritually and emotionally. He has given you the power to choose joy. To trust Him. And to be a blessing to your husband. Even if your spouse isn't your soul mate, you can still choose to respond positively to him. A joyful life doesn't begin with perfect circumstances. It begins with how you respond to those circumstances. And you get to decide your response every day.

Choose to Focus on Your Spiritual Blessings

You Are a Friend of God

Sitting at my computer, I sang along with a worship CD at the top of my lungs. "I am a friend of God, He calls me friend." I wanted to get up, dance around the kitchen, and clap my hands. If you want to cultivate joy, think about what this biblical truth is saying: We have a never-changing relationship with God that is given to us for our blessing. We are His friends!

He is a friend who won't ever fail you (John 15:14-15). He is for you and wants your best. He is at work in your life (Romans 8:31-32). Because God has reconciled you to Himself through Christ, you can confidently declare, "I am a friend of God" (cf. 2 Corinthians 5:18-19). "May the God of hope fill you with all joy and peace as you trust in him," Pauls tells us in Romans 15:13. By faith in Jesus, by receiving Him as your Savior, you are forever His friend (John 1:12).

To thrive when things are difficult between you and your husband, focus your mind on these truths, not your problems.

You Are Indwelt by His Spirit

Every desire you have to please God by working on your marriage is from Him. His Spirit fills you, causing you to want what He wants.

You might wonder what it means to be indwelt or filled with the Spirit. Or what connection this has with understanding and accepting your spouse.

> Every desire you have to please God by
> working on your marriage is from Him.

Is being filled a feeling? An ecstatic experience? Or a doctrine that leaves you puzzled? Scripture tells us to continuously "be filled with the Spirit" (Ephesians 5:18). But how do you know if this is true of you at any given time? Here are some ways to find out:

- *Check what you're thinking and feeling.* What do you tell yourself about your husband? Does it reflect love? Show patience? Display self-control? These are the marks of being filled with the Spirit—especially when you're at odds with each other (Galatians 5:22).

- *Look at how you relate to your husband.* Do you insist on having your way on most issues? Or do you respond to him with God-given consideration, kindness, and gentleness?

- *Consider your desires and prayers.* How do they reflect the Spirit's presence in you?

When you invite God's Spirit to continuously fill you, you want to live under His authority. You want to please Him. You want your life to show evidence that He is alive in you. In turn, you will experience the joy of the Lord flowing through you and blessing your marriage.

You Have His Word

This is going to sound blunt, but it is true: we can all come up with reasons for not feeding on God's Word. However, if you don't read Scripture, take the time to think about its meaning and pray it into your heart, you won't thrive and experience the joy of the Lord. Why is this? Because God's Word is a guidebook, a life-coaching manual that shows you what builds a strong marriage and what tears it down.

The Bible contains countless principles that both deepen your walk with the Lord and build your marriage. For example, in Psalm 119:9-16, the writer asks, "How can I keep my life pure, not just sexually but also from selfishness, a me-first attitude, greed, grudges, and pride?" (Poppy's paraphrase). In other words, how can I live a life that brings joy to God? Here are some of his answers:

- v. 9—Live according to God's Word. It isn't that complicated.

- v. 10—Seek God with all your heart.

- v. 10—Depend on God, asking for help not to stray from His commands.

- v. 11—Hide God's Word in your heart. Start memorizing His promises or the truths you need to keep remembering.

- v. 11—Make inner change your motivation for memorizing Scripture.

- v. 12—Ask God to teach you what He wants you to know.

- v. 13—Rejoice in following God. It is a great way to live a positive and productive life.

- v. 15—Consider, think about, and meditate on what God says and the greatness of who He is.

- v. 16—Delight in God's decrees. He intends them for good, to bless and energize your life.

- v. 16—Intentionally make time for reading Scripture. Refuse to neglect it.

David declared, "My shield is God Most High" (Psalm 7:10). He was conscious that no matter how clever or strong he was in battle, his ultimate safety rested in God's protection. In the spiritual attacks that come against every Christian marriage, our shield is also found in God Most High.

Paul reinforces the importance of remembering that God is our protector against the attacks of Satan and "the spiritual forces of evil in the heavenly realms." When the enemy comes against us, he instructs, "stand firm" and "take up the shield of faith." By knowing God's Word, you can use it to combat all that Satan throws against your heart and mind. You don't have to be overcome by his fiery darts of fear, despair, and doubt (Ephesians 6:10-19).

Why read the Bible? Because if you don't, you will miss the powerful insights, truths, encouragement, and guidance that God longs to give you.

Choose to Cherish Your Husband

Barbara Bush, wife of former president George H.W. Bush says, "At the end of your life you will never regret not having passed one more test, not winning one more verdict, or not closing one more deal. You will regret time not spent with a husband, a friend, a child, or a parent."

Learning to cherish your husband, even if you don't see eye-to-eye on various issues, will produce more joy in your marriage than complaining. It's a matter of training yourself to look beyond what irritates you and to appreciate his good points

Karen Whiting, an author and speaker, used to fume when her

husband arrived home late. She knew he was spending time listening to someone else's problems. Her caring husband was always available if people wanted to talk.

"One evening as I was angry yet again," Karen said, "I picked up my Bible and noticed how Jesus always stopped and paid attention to people's needs. I thought about how I had dated Jim because he was so kind and nonjudgmental. I realized I didn't want to change him. What I had selfishly wanted was for him to just come home and be with me. I'm thankful for Jim's example. It helped me admit that I need to learn from him and become a better listener."

In spite of our differences, I've also learned some helpful lessons from my husband. Following his father's example, Jim keeps his promises without fail and never lies under any circumstance. In my home, it was okay to tell little white lies to get out of things you didn't want to do. So was backing out of commitments if you changed your mind.

I had no problem making up excuses. After all, what was wrong with an innocent fib if it didn't harm anyone? As I grew in my walk with God, I saw this had to change. But old habits can pop up at unexpected times.

Wanting to get out of a commitment to teach a Bible study for a year, I told Jim I was going to call and make an excuse.

"You can't do that," he said. "You gave your word."

We talked about what I wanted to do many times, but Jim remained adamant. In the end, I recognized that God had given me a husband with integrity because I needed a character adjustment.

To thrive in your marriage, work on cultivating a positive attitude toward your husband. Think about his worthwhile qualities. And ask yourself, how have his good qualities helped me grow in some area of my character?

> To thrive in your marriage, work on cultivating
> a positive attitude toward your husband.

Take time to thank the Lord for the specific man He gave you. And while you're thinking about your husband's good points, look for practical ways to express your appreciation.

Choose to Flourish

In her life-affirming book, *Flourish,* Catherine Hart Weber writes, "We flourish when we have a sense of well-being and can function positively in our spiritual, personal, and social lives. Flourishing means we are able to have close relationships and a meaningful and purposeful life."[1]

Although your marriage might be less than ideal, God's desire is for you to flourish, to thrive, to choose to be happy. He wants you to enjoy your life. It is a gift from Him. The psalmist describes this truth with a promise: "The godly shall flourish like palm trees and grow tall as the cedars of Lebanon. For they are transplanted into the Lord's own garden" (Psalm 92:12-13 TLB).

In order to thrive, cultivate a joy-filled heart. Here's how this can be your experience:

- Joy comes when you focus on God's ability to provide what you need rather than allowing yourself to be dragged down by a spirit of despair.

- Joy comes when you fill your heart with God's promises, making your faith soar with the confidence that you are never alone.

- Joy comes when you trust God, look beyond yourself, and choose to be a blessing to others.

- Joy comes when you seek the Lord for strength to love your husband.

My goal in this book has been to help you understand why you and your husband are not alike and to point out some legitimate reasons for your differences. I hope the stories, quizzes, and Scriptures have provided many aha moments and encouraged you to invite the Lord to keep working in your marriage. My longing and prayer is that this book has equipped and inspired you to keep growing into the woman God knows you can become.

May I Pray for You?

Lord Jesus, I ask You to help my friend choose to walk in love toward her spouse. Flood her with feelings of love toward him. Keep her from wrapping all her hopes of happiness around an imperfect person. May she delight Your heart as she fixes her hope on You, the only One who is perfect, the only One who knows her intimately and can meet her deepest needs. Give her abundant joy, Lord. May she thrive as Your child whether or not her husband ever becomes more like her! Amen.

Notes

Chapter One: What Happened to My Dreams?

1. Gary Thomas, *Sacred Marriage* (Grand Rapids, MI: Zondervan, 2000), 14.

2. "Divorce Statistics and Trend," *Love-Sessions*, www.love-sessions.com/divorcestatistics.htm.

3. Ibid.

4. David Popenoe, "Debunking 10 Divorce Myths," *Discovery Fit and Health*, http:health.how stuffworks.com/relationships/marriage/debunking-divorce-myths5.htm.

5. Sara Eleoff, "An Exploration of the Ramifications of Divorce on Children and Adolescents," *Child Advocate*, www.childadvocate.net/divorce_effects_on_children.htm.

6. www.ahealth.com/consumer/disorders/childrendivorce.html.

7. Popenoe, "Debunking 10 Divorce Myths."

8. Ibid.

9. Thomas, *Sacred Marriage,* 128.

Chapter Two: Facing Crossroads—Making Choices

1. Charles Stanley, *The Source of My Strength* (Nashville, TN: Thomas Nelson Inc., 1994), 139.

2. Ibid., 140.

3. Poppy Smith, *I'm Too Human to Be Like Jesus* (Belleville, Ontario, Canada: Essence Publishing, 2006).

Chapter Three: He's Not My Clone!

1. "Cloning Fact Sheet," Human Genome Project Information, www.ornl.gov/sci/techresources /Human Genome/elsi/cloning.shtml#humans.

2. Val Farmer, "Rural, Urban Differences Interesting," July 25, 2003, www.kiowacountypress .com/2003-07/07-25/Urban,%20Rural%20Differences%20Interesting.htm.

3. Leslie Vernick, *The Emotionally Destructive Relationship* (Eugene, OR: Harvest House Publishers, 2007), 27-28.

Chapter Four: We Weren't Raised in the Same Home

1. P. Roger Hillerstrom, *Your Family Voyage* (Grand Rapids, MI: Fleming H. Revell, 1993), 13.

2. David H. Olson, Amy Olson-Sigg, and Peter J. Larson, *The Couple Checkup* (Nashville, TN: Thomas Nelson, 2008), 127.

3. Ibid., 137.

4. Susan Forward, *Toxic Parents* (New York, NY: Bantam Books, 1989), 6.

5. Ibid., 174.

Chapter Five: His Brain Isn't Wired Like Mine

1. Walt Larimore and Barb Larimore, *His Brain, Her Brain* (Grand Rapids, MI: Zondervan, 2008), 33-36.

2. Ibid., 45-47.

3. Ibid., 47.

4. Barbara and Allan Pease, *Why Men Don't Listen and Women Can't Read Maps* (Mona Vale, NSW, Australia: Pease Training International, 1998), 21.

5. Larimore and Larimore, *His Brain, Her Brain*, 50.

6. Ibid., 51.

7. Ibid.

8. Pease, *Why Men Don't Listen*, 180.

9. David H. Olson, Amy Olson-Sigg, and Peter J. Larson, *The Couple Checkup* (Nashville, TN: Thomas Nelson, 2008), 214.

10. Ibid., 214.

Chapter Six: We Don't Have the Same Emotional Needs

1. John Eldredge, *Wild at Heart* (Nashville, TN: Thomas Nelson, 2001), 8.

2. David H. Olson, Amy Olson-Sigg, and Peter J. Larson, *The Couple Checkup* (Nashville, TN: Thomas Nelson, 2008), 17.

3. Willard F. Harley Jr., *His Needs, Her Needs* (Old Tappan, NJ: Fleming H. Revell, 1996), 29.

4. Ibid., 35.

5. "Lonely Hearts Club," *Better Homes and Gardens,* August 2010, 206.

6. Harley, *His Needs, Her Needs,* 98.

7. Rebecca Cutter, *When Opposites Attract* (New York, NY: Penguin Books, 1994), 131.

Chapter Seven: When I Say This, He Hears That

1. David H. Olson, Amy Olson-Sigg, and Peter J. Larson, *The Couple Checkup* (Nashville, TN: Thomas Nelson, 2008), 34.

2. Deborah Tannen, *Talking From 9 to 5* (New York, NY: Harper Collins, 1995).

3. Barbara and Allan Pease, *Why Men Don't Listen and Women Can't Read Maps* (Mona Vale, NSW, Australia: Pease Training International, 1998), 145.

4. http://mid4.net/category/malefemale-jokes/.

5. www.mikeysfunnies.com, April 19, 2011.

6. Florence and Marita Littauer, *Getting Along with Almost Anybody* (Grand Rapids, MI: Fleming H. Revell, 1998), 28.

7. Sandra Gray Bender, *Recreating Marriage with the Same Old Spouse* (Louisville, KY: Westminster John Knox Press, 1997), 111.

Chapter Eight: He Handles Conflict One Way, I Handle It Another

1. Neil and Joanne Anderson, *Daily in Christ* (Eugene, OR: Harvest House Publishers, 1993), April 7.

2. Florence and Marita Littauer, *Getting Along with Almost Anybody* (Grand Rapids, MI: Fleming H. Revell, 1998), 41.

3. John Gottman, Cliff Notarius, Jonni Gonso, and Howard Markman, *A Couple's Guide to Communication* (Champaign, IL: Research Press, 1976), 89.

4. Ibid., 6.

5. Leslie Vernick, *The Emotionally Destructive Relationship* (Eugene, OR: Harvest House Publishers, 2007), 27.

Chapter Nine: I Think "Bargain," He Thinks "Bankruptcy"

1. "Kiss Spats Goodbye," *Self,* March 2011, 101.

2. http://EzineArticles.com/?expert=JoeLarson.

3. Kay Bell, "Divorce 101: Restoring Your Finances," *MSN*, May 26. 2009, http://articles.money central.msn.com/CollegeAndFamily/SuddenlySingle/Divorce101RestoringYourFinances.aspx.

4. www.statcon.gc.ca/pub/82-003-x/2006005/article/marital-conjugal/4060665-eng.htm.

5. Dana Hinders, "Divorce Statistics," *Love to Know*, http://divorce.lovetoknow.com/Divorce Statistics.

6. Gary L. McIntosh and Samuel D. Rima, *Overcoming the Dark Side of Leadership* (Grand Rapids, MI: Baker Books, 1997), 74.

7. http://articles.moneycentral.msn.com/Investing/StockInvestingTrading/WhatsYourMoneyPersonality.aspx#pageTopAnchor.

8. Vivian Baniak in Florence and Marita Littauer, *Getting Along with Almost Anybody* (Grand Rapids, MI: Fleming H. Revell, 1998), 228.

9. Ibid.

10. http://articles.moneycentral.msn.com./Investing/StockInvestingTrading/WhatsYourMoneyPersonlity.aspx#pageTopAnchor.

11. David H. Olson, Amy Olson-Sigg, and Peter J. Larson, *The Couple Checkup* (Nashville, TN: Thomas Nelson, 2008), 93.

12. Jimmy Evans, *Marriage on the Rock* (Amarillo, TX: Majestic Media, 1996), 233.

Chapter Ten: We're Not on the Same Page Spiritually

1. David H. Olson, Amy Olson-Sigg, and Peter J. Larson, *The Couple Checkup* (Nashville, TN: Thomas Nelson, 2008), 147.

2. Nick Harrison, *Magnificent Prayer* (Grand Rapids, MI: Zondervan, 2001), 228.

3. David Murrow, *Why Men Hate Going to Church* (Nashville, TN: Thomas Nelson, 2005), 16.

4. Marita Littauer with Betty Southard, *Your Spiritual Personality* (San Francisco, CA: Jossey-Bass, 2005).

5. Gary Thomas, *Sacred Pathways* (Grand Rapids, MI: Zondervan, 2006), 16.

Chapter Eleven: We Get "Headaches" for Different Reasons

1. Gary Thomas, *Sacred Marriage* (Grand Rapids, MI: Zondervan, 2000), 224.

2. Joe S. McIlhaney Jr. and Freda McKissic Bush, *Hooked: New Science on How Casual Sex Is Affecting Our Children* (Chicago: Northfield Publishing, 2008), quoted in Ed Vitagliano, "Bonded in the Brain," *American Family Journal*, October 2010, 14-15.

3. Michele Weiner-Davis, "Is Your Marriage Sex-Starved?" www.divorcebusting.com/sexquiz.htm.

4. "National Review: Getting Serious on Pornography," *NPR*, March 31, 2010, www.npr.org/templates/story/story.php?storyId=125382361.

5. Ian Kerner, quoted in Jenna McCarthy, "Steal His Mojo!" *Self.com,* July 2010, 96.

6. Les Parrott, quoted in ibid., 95.

7. Steven R. Tracy, *Mending the Soul* (Grand Rapids, MI: Zondervan, 2005), 122.

8. Sandra Gray Bender, *Recreating Marriage with the Same Old Spouse* (Louisville, KY: Westminster John Knox Press, 1997), 12-13.

9. Gary Thomas, *Sacred Marriage* (Grand Rapids, MI: Zondervan, 2006), 196.

Chapter Twelve: Choose to Thrive

1. Catherine Hart Weber, *Flourish* (Bloomington, MN: Bethany House, 2010), 19.

About the Author

Poppy Smith is British, married to an American, and has lived in many countries. She brings an international flair seasoned with humorous honesty as she illustrates biblical truths. A former Bible Study Fellowship teaching leader with a master's degree in spiritual formation, Poppy speaks at retreats, conferences, and special events around the world. She challenges Christians to look at their choices, attitudes, and relationship with God.

Poppy's books include the bestselling *I'm Too Young to Be This Old, I'm Too Human to Be Like Jesus*, and *Reaching Higher: Ten Dynamic Truths from Abraham that Will Transform Your Life*. Poppy has also authored two Bible studies: *Wisdom for Today's Woman* and *Speaking Wisely, Exploring the Power of Words*. Her monthly e-zine, *Thrive*, touches many lives with inspiring principles for spiritual and personal growth.

To find out more or to contact Poppy, visit her website at

www.poppysmith.com

To learn more about other Harvest House books
or to read sample chapters, log on to our website:

www.harvesthousepublishers.com

HARVEST HOUSE PUBLISHERS
EUGENE, OREGON